Oscar Wilde

Sunflower Edition

THE WORKS
OF
OSCAR WILDE

HIS LIFE

WITH A CRITICAL ESTIMATE
OF HIS WRITINGS

ILLUSTRATED

NEW YORK
LAMB PUBLISHING CO.
MCMIX

53464

CONTENTS.

CHAPTER		PAGE
I.	The Parents of Oscar Wilde	1
II.	Home, School and University Life . .	31
III.	Early London Life	53
IV.	American Lectures	73
V.	First Sojourn in Paris	135
VI.	Lectures in Great Britain . . .	159
VII.	Marriage	173
VIII.	The Picture of Dorian Gray . . .	196
IX.	Plays and Prosperity . . .	233
X.	From the French of Andre Gide . .	255
XI.	A Literary Estimate	273

ILLUSTRATIONS.

PAGE

Oscar Wilde (1883)....................*Frontispiece*

Portora Royal School 64

Royal Eye and Ear Hospital..................... 128

No. 16 Tite Street............................... 192

Oscar Wilde's Grave at Bagneux.................. 255

INTRODUCTION

The reaction which has so steadily set in within the last year or two as regards the literary remains of Oscar Wilde calls persistently for a complete edition of his works. The verdict of the posterity of to-day—that alien homage which the prophet unhonored in his own country receives from the stranger abroad—has reacted upon the present generation at home and has replaced Wilde's statue on that pedestal in the domestic Pantheon whence it had fallen, as men deemed forever.

On the Continent there is no stronger exotic influence than that of Wilde upon much of the literature of to-day, and both England and America are waking to the fact that Wilde is among the immortals in literature whose works cannot be allowed to die.

It is to preserve these works in their entirety that this complete edition was designed. In the case of Oscar Wilde, Shakespeare's oft quoted couplet may be reversed—the good that he did lives after him, the evil is interred with his bones.

The biography itself is mainly a compilation from the writings of men who knew Wilde personally; also, newspapers and other publications of his time have been drawn upon, and these latter, after careful search, have revealed some interesting material.

The facts in the life of Wilde that are primarily related to his literary work are the ones that have been specially dwelt upon, and much matter of a critical nature pertaining to this work has been embodied in the biography.

In preparing this edition of the works of Oscar Wilde great care has been exercised in the selection of the material. Already a considerable amount of apocryphal literature has been accredited to Wilde, and in order to exclude this everything included in this edition has been carefully scrutinized by close students of the writings of Oscar Wilde. Wherever internal evidence of thought and style points to Wilde as the author, such work has been included in this edition. For it has been thought wiser to include writings which future scholarship, basing its conclusions upon external evidence not now available, may pronounce clever forgeries, than to take the chance of excluding work really by the hand of Wilde.

THE LIFE OF OSCAR WILDE.

CHAPTER I.

THE PARENTS OF OSCAR WILDE.

"Mr. Wilde," said Bernard Shaw in the heyday of his compatriot's career, "is almost as acutely Irish an Irishman as the Iron Duke of Wellington." This epigram is hardly as clever as might have been expected from a critic of Shaw's reputation, for it contains something of an anticlimax. Coming of the same class of well-born Irishmen, which has given to England not only her greatest soldiers but also her most brilliant statesmen and orators and her most beloved poets, Oscar Wilde, rather than the Duke, should have been taken as the standard of comparison, for Wilde had it within his intellectual and temperamental power to have become a master spirit in whatever field of endeavor he chose. Gifted

1

with a good presence, a voice of golden sweetness, instinctive felicity in the choice of spoken as well as of written words, an analytic mind, an unerring artistic taste, and, above all, a keen perception of humor, his was such a personality as imagination loves to deck with the play-finery of "what might have been." Had he inherited, in addition to her other intellectual and spiritual legacies, his mother's patriotism, he might have stood before England and the world as another O'Connell, the Irish tribune, or, more probably, might have been hanged like Emmet, with some splendid, bold defiance on his lips. Place him, even, in the boots of the Iron Duke, and, while his fate of climacteric downfall would probably have followed him, he would in some paradoxical fashion have gained *éclat* even from defeat.

No one more clearly recognized his capability of great deeds than Wilde himself. He deliberately chose a career the limitations and debilitating tendencies of which were patent to his prescient soul. Thus in the sonnet which he chose for the foreword of his poems he bursts forth in an outcry of passionate regret, the sincerity of which removes every suggestion of self-adulation:

HELAS!

To drift with every passion till my soul
  Is a stringed lute on which all winds can play,
  Is it for this that I have given away
Mine ancient wisdom and austere control?
Methinks my life is a twice-written scroll
  Scrawled over on some boyish holiday,
  With idle songs for pipe and virelay,
Which do but mar the secret of the whole.
  Surely there was a time I might have trod
The sunlit heights, and from life's dissonance
  Struck one clear chord to reach the ear of God:
  Is that time dead? lo! with a little rod
I did but touch the honey of romance—
And must I lose a soul's inheritance?

That his parents, especially his mother, had high
ambitions for him, hoping that he would become a
great Irish patriot, is indicated by the names they
gave him: "Oscar Fingal O'Flahertie Wills Wilde."
Although on arriving at years of discretion he
chose to be known simply as "Oscar Wilde,"
in his callow youth he wrote his name in full, evidently with great family pride.

Oscar might well be proud of his father, William

Robert Wills Wilde (born in 1815, died in 1876), who was the most famous surgeon of Ireland, and a specialist in diseases of the eye and ear of international fame and practice. The German scientists accorded him the highest praise for his perfect command of the most delicate situation in the operating room, and for his unerring and instant deductions in difficult cases, indicating that he possessed the inspiration of genius which asserts itself no less in professional pursuits than in literature and the arts. Many stories are told of his quick resourcefulness, of which one, related by Sherard, will suffice for illustration:

"Sir William once saved the sight of a Dublin fisherman, who was brought to him with a darning-needle embedded up to the head in his right eye. The flapping of a sail in which the needle was sticking had driven it in with terrible force. An ordinary operation was out of the question; there was not enough of the head protruding to allow of any hold being got on it with a forceps by which it might have been drawn from its place. The man was suffering terrible agony. Sir William saw at once what was the only means of extracting the needle. He sent for a powerful electro-magnet, by the help of which in the shortest time the steel bar was extracted."

Dr. Wilde was especially noted for his knowledge of the ear. Dr. Swarze, an eminent German scientist, called him, with the unanimous approbation of the medical world, "The Father of Modern Otology." Dr. Wilde was honored by royalty both at home and abroad. In 1853 he was made Surgeon-Oculist-in-Ordinary to the Queen of England, the first appointment of the kind made in Ireland. On the occasion of his visit to Stockholm in 1857, the King of Sweden created him Chevalier of the Kingdom of Sweden, and decorated him with the Order of the Polar Star.

But medical renown and royal honors, even the great pecuniary rewards that came to him from the outset of his career, did not enter into his purpose in practising his profession. A pure and disinterested love for the art of healing was the great passion of his life.

During the first year of his practice (1841) Dr. Wilde devoted his entire earnings, a matter of £400, to the establishment of a charitable eye and ear hospital in Dublin, and thereafter gave not only a large part of his time to the management of the institution, but also contributed a large por-

tion of his income. It was the only institution of
its kind, not only in the city, but in all Ireland,
and no man can reckon the benefit of such an
endowment.

The stable wherein the hospital was started gave
place in time to a proper building, known as St.
Mark's Ophthalmic Hospital, and this was finally
amalgamated with the National Eye and Ear In-
firmary, started some time after the foundation of
St. Mark's, the two forming the present Royal Victoria Eye and Ear Hospital, the undeserved and
supplanting name being most significant of the
ingratitude of monarchies. It should be added,
however, that in the hall of the hospital stands a
bust of Sir William Wilde, bought at bargain price
at a sale of the effects of his son "Willy," after the
death of the unfortunate young man.

The first annual report of the institution, issued
in 1844, recites the facts of its establishment and
its early services to humanity, and, in justice to
the neglected memory of one of Ireland's greatest
benefactors, is here in part reproduced:

"Although most of the large hospitals in this
city and the several infirmaries, poorhouses, and
other institutions in Ireland which afford indoor

medical relief admit patients labouring under af-
fections of the organs of sight and hearing, there
has not up to the present period existed in this
country any special hospital for treating the diseases of the eye and ear.

"The want of such an establishment, upon a
scale so extensive as to afford general relief, has
long been felt by the poor, and is generally acknowledged by the upper classes of society. . . . In
the year 1841 a dispensary for treating the dis-
seases of these organs was established in South
Frederick Lane, and supported by its founder, Sir
William Wilde, for twelve months; at the end of
which time, finding the number of applicants and
the consequent expenditure far exceeding what was
originally contemplated, or what could be supported by individual exertion, and not wishing to
apply for public aid for the sum required to defray
its expenses, he determined to try the experiment
of making it support itself, by a monthly subscrip-
tion from each of the patients. This plan succeeded fully, and since September, 1842, the patients have each paid a small monthly sum during
the period of their attendance, which has defrayed
the expenses of the medicine. In this way 1,056
persons were treated during the year ending Sep-

tember, 1843, and the total number of patients relieved with medicine, medical advice, or by operation from the commencement of that institution to the 1st of March, 1844, was 2,075. Paupers have, however, at all times received advice and medicine gratuitously. The sum paid by each patient is but sixpence per month, and this system of partial payments has been found to work exceedingly well. It has produced care, regularity and attention, and induced a spirit of independence among the lower orders of society worthy of countenance and support, while the annual sum of £50 received in this way is in itself a sufficient guarantee . . . that its benefits are appreciated by the poor, numbers of whom seek its advantages from distant parts of the country."

In his private affairs, as well as in his professional services, Dr. Wilde was a practical philanthropist. He solved individually the problem of Irish landlordism along lines that have since proved successful as a state policy. He purchased an estate where the tenantry were in a wretched state, exceptional even in Ireland, owing to surplus population. He paid the more miserable of the peasants to move away, gave those remaining ampler tenant rights, and hired them to make extensive improvements on the estate. A contemporary account of these reforms is here reproduced, not only because it reflects honor upon Dr. Wilde, but also because it indicates the source of his son Oscar's humane and practical social philosophy:

"Some years ago Sir William Wilde became a proprietor in the county of Mayo, where he has most successfully carried out schemes of improvement, and has shown that he can reclaim land and profitably carry on farming operations, which is what few of even resident proprietors can boast. Finding a portion of the ancestral estate of the O'Flyns (from whom he is maternally descended) for sale in the Land Estate Court, he became the purchaser. The portion in cultivation was covered by a wretched pauper tenantry, numbers of whom it became necessary to remove to enable those remaining to have a means of comfortable existence. Understanding somewhat of the language of the people, and, being, as they said, 'one of the ould stock,' he was able with advice from the Catholic clergy to carry out his plans without exciting discontent or involving the sacrifice of large sums of money, and he gave an ample tenant right to

those that remained on the property over twelve
years ago. The reclamation that followed, with the
addition of erecting a residence for himself in a
most picturesque situation, has converted a locality
characterised only a few years ago by the usual
evidences of neglect, into one of the most attractive and charming spots in the country. In fact,
Mayhera House, near Cong, with the surrounding
grounds and estate, may be fairly claimed as one
of the numerous triumphs of the enterprising proprietor."

Dr. Wilde was also distinguished in the field
of scholarship. From his boyhood he was interested in the legendary lore and archæology of his
native island. During his school days, which he
spent at the Royal School of Banagher, he was wont
to run away on fishing excursions to talk with the
peasantry and explore the ruins of ancient Irish
civilization.

Of these days a contributor to the *Dublin University Magazine* writes as follows:

"The delight of the fisher lad was to spend his
time on the banks of the lakes and rivers within
his. reach, talk Irish with the people, and listen

to the recital of Irish legends and tales; his knowledge of which he so well turned to account in the 'Irish Popular Superstitions.' His taste for antiquarian research was early exhibited, and much fostered by his repeated examinations of the cahirs, forts and caves of the early Irish which exist in the vicinity of Castlerea, as well as by visits to the plain of Ruthcragan, the site of the great palace and cemetery of the chieftains of the West. In the district around were castles, whose legends he learned; patterns, where he witnessed the strange mixture of pilgrimage, devotion, fun and frolic; cockfights, for which Roscommon was then famous; and the various superstitions and ceremonies connected with the succession of the festivals of the season—all these made a deep impression on the romantic nature of young Wilde, and many of them have been handed down to posterity by his facile pen."

During his lifetime Dr. Wilde published a number of works on Irish archæology, history and legend. He founded the *Dublin Quarterly Journal of Science*. At the time of his death, which occurred April 19, 1876, he was engaged on a life of Béranger. This work was completed by Lady Wilde,

who embraced the opportunity of paying the tribute
of a scholar as well as a wife by saying in the
preface:

"There was probably no man of his generation
more versed in our national literature, in all that
concerned the land and the people, the arts, architecture, topography, statistics, and even the legends
of the country; but, above all, in his favourite department, the descriptive illustration of Ireland,
past and present, in historic and prehistoric times,
he has justly gained a wide reputation, as one of
the most learned and accurate, and at the same
time one of the most popular writers of the age
on Irish subjects . . . in the misty cloudland
of Irish antiquities he may especially be looked
upon as a safe and steadfast guide."

It was even more from his mother than his
father that Oscar Wilde derived his artistic temperament and literary inclination. Jane Francesca
Elgee (born in 1826, died in 1896) won in early
womanhood a reputation wherever an Irish heart
pulsed with patriotic ardor for his native land,
by her fervent advocacy in poetry and prose of
the Nationalist cause, written under the pen name

of "Speranza." The following review of her poems presents something of the effect they had in firing the very inflammable Irish heart of those burning days:

POEMS BY "SPERANZA."

[From critical article entitled "Recent Irish Poetry" in the *Dublin Review*. The poems were published by Duffy, of Dublin, 1864.]

"These poems, if full justice is to be done to them, ought to be read from first to last with a running commentary in the memory from the history of those few tragic years whose episodes they in a manner mark. One poem is a mournfully passionate appeal to O'Connell against the alliance with the Whigs, which was charged as one of the causes of the secession. Another is a ballad of the famine, with lights as ghastly as ever glowed in the imagination of Euripides or Dante, and founded on horrors such as Greek or Italian never witnessed. . . . Again, a glowing series of images recalls to us the awful state of the country—the corpses that were buried without coffins, and the men and women that walked the roads more like corpses than living creatures, spectres and skeletons at once; the little children out of whose sunken eyes the very tears were dried, and over whose bare little bones the hideous fur of famine had begun to grow; the cholera cart, with its load of helpless, huddled humanity, on its way to the hospital; the emigrant ship sending back its woeful wail of farewell from swarming poop to stern in the offing; and, far as the eye could search the land, the blackened potato-fields, filling all the air with the fetid odours of decay. Again and again such pictures are contrasted with passionate lyrics full of rebellious fire, urging the people to die, if die they must, by the sword rather than by hunger. . . .

"It is a curious fact, and reminds one of the myth of Achilles' heel, that O'Connell, who marched among his myriad foes like one clad in panoply of mail from head to foot, with a sort of expugnable vigour and endurance, not to be wounded, not to be stunned, with his buckler ready for every blow that rained on his casque, was weak as a child under the influence of verse. . . .

"These lines of 'Speranza,' which appeared in the *Nation* at the time of the secession, stung him to the very heart:

Gone from us—dead to us—he whom we wor-
    shipped so!
  Low lies the altar we raised to his name;
Madly his own hand hath shattered and laid it
    low—
  Madly his own breath hath blasted his fame.
He whose proud bosom once raged with humanity,
  He whose broad forehead was circled with might;
Sunk to a time-serving, drivelling inanity—
  God! why not spare our loved country the sight?

Was it the gold of the stranger that tempted him?
  Ah! we'd have pledged to him body and soul—
Toiled for him—fought for him—starved for him
    —died for him—
  Smiled though our graves were the steps to his
    goal.
Breathed he one word in his deep, earnest whisper-
    ing,
  Wealth, crown, and kingdom were laid at his
    feet;
Raised he his right hand, the millions would round
    him cling—
  Hush! 'tis the Sassenach ally you greet.

It is well to add to this excellent illustration

of "Speranza's" truly Irish command of scathing invective one of her poems expressive of that even more characteristic Irish trait—sublime confidence in the triumph of justice:

RESURGAM.

The sunshine falls
Upon ruined walls
And the desolate places lying
Like a desert vast
Of ruin and waste
Strewn with wrecks of the dead and dying.
And the exile roams
From the roofless homes
Of his own fair, beautiful islet,
With never a care
In his dull despair
Where the winds or the waves may pilot.

Yet the fever strife
Of a Nation's life
Is a fearful thing and a splendid,
For through storm and night
The glory and light
Of the coming of day is blended.

The cry of despair
In the silent air,
So helpless it seems, and feeble:
But the dying groans
May have shaken thrones
From the lips of a murdered people.

Great thoughts will move
In the mighty groove
Of a nation travelling onward,
As the fiery flood
Of the wrath of God
When the whirlwind is sweeping downward.
And the chanted song
Of a Nation's wrong
To the low, sweet chords of the player,
Can sever the chain
Of the slave in twain,
Like the hammer of Thor, the Slayer.

For our right is might
In the deadly fight
We wage with the powers of Evil,
And our thunder-words
Are like lifted swords
To war against man or devil.

Lo ! the path we tread
By our martyred dead
Has been trodden 'mid bane and blessing,
But unconquered still
Is the steadfast will
And the faith they died confessing.

SPERANZA.

Lady Wilde has related how she came to enter into the Nationalist movement:

"Till my eighteenth year, I never wrote anything. Then, one day, a volume of 'Ireland's Library,' issued from *The Nation* office by Mr. Duffy, happened to come my way. I read it eagerly, and my patriotism was kindled. [This volume was D'Alton Williams' book, "The Spirit of the Nation."] Till then I was quite indifferent to the National movement, and if I thought about it at all, probably had a bad opinion of its leaders. For my family was Protestant and Conservative, and there was no social intercourse between them and the Catholics and Nationalists. But once I had caught the National spirit, and all the literature of Irish songs and sufferings had an enthralling interest for me, then it was that I discovered that I could write poetry. In sending my verses to the editor of *The Nation* I dared not have my name published, so I signed them 'Speranza,' and my letters 'John Fenshaw Ellis,' instead of Jane Francesca Elgee."

Miss Elgee became a national heroine as well as national poetess through her bravery in rising in open court and confessing that she was the author of an unsigned seditious article, for publishing which in his paper, *The Nation,* Charles Duffy was being prosecuted. During the trial she rose in the gallery and cried: "I am the culprit, if culprit there be." The bravery of this confession appealed to the gallantry of the Irish jurymen, and they disagreed, with the result that the editor was discharged, and no prosecution instituted against his fellow "culprit."

It is here reproduced as a typical revolutionary appeal of the time, as well as an illustration of the bold spirit that was imbibed with his mother's milk by the man of whom his brother said, when all but members of his family urged him to flee the country before certain disgrace, "Oscar is an Irish gentleman. He will face the music."

JACTA EST ALEA.*

"The Irish Nation has at length decided. England has done us one good service at least. Her recent acts have taken away the last miserable pretext for passive submission. She has justified us before the world, and ennobled the timid, humble supplication of a degraded, insulted people, into the proud demand for independence by a resolved, prepared, and fearless Nation.

"Now, indeed, were the men of Ireland *cowards* if this moment for retribution, combat, and victory were to pass by unemployed. It finds them slaves, but it would leave them infamous.

"Oh! for a hundred thousand muskets glittering brightly in the light of heaven, and the monumental barricades stretching across each of our noble streets, made desolate by England—circling round that doomed Castle, made infamous by England, where the foregone tyrant has held his council

*"The die is cast," or the "throw is made," a gambling expression indicating unalterable committal to an act and its results, said to have been uttered by Julius Cæsar when he led his army across the river Rubicon into Pompey's territory.

of treason and iniquity against our people and our country for seven hundred years.

"Courage rises with danger, and heroism with resolve. Does not our breath come freer, each heart beat quicker in these rare and grand moments of human life, when all doubt, and wavering, and weakness are cast to the winds, and the soul rises majestic over each petty obstacle, each low, selfish consideration, and, flinging off the fetters of prejudice, bigotry, and egotism, bounds forward into the higher, diviner life of heroism and patriotism, defiant as a conqueror, devoted as a martyr, omnipotent as a Deity!

"We appeal to the whole Irish Nation—is there any man amongst us who wishes to take one further step on the base path of sufferance and slavery? Is there one man that thinks that Ireland has not been sufficiently insulted, that Ireland has not been sufficiently degraded in her honour and her rights, to justify her now in fiercely turning upon her oppressor? No! a man so infamous cannot tread the earth; or, if he does, the voice of the coward is stifled in the clear, wild, ringing shout that leaps from hill to hill, that echoes from sea to sea, that peals from the lips of an uprisen Nation—'We must be free!'

"In the name then of your trampled, insulted, degraded country; in the name of all heroic virtues, of all that makes life illustrious or death divine; in the name of your starved, your exiled, your *dead;* by your martyrs in prison cells and felon chains; in the name of God and man; by the listening earth and the watching heaven, I call on you to make this aspiration of your souls a *deed.* Even as you read these weak words of a heart that yet palpitates with an enthusiasm as heroic as your own, and your breast heaves and your eyes grow dim with tears as the memory of Ireland's wrongs rushes upon your soul—even now lift up your right hand to heaven and swear—swear by your undying soul, by your hopes of immortality, never to lay down your arms, never to cease hostilities, till you regenerate and save this fallen land.

"Gather round the standard of your chiefs. Who dares to say he will not follow when O'Brien leads? Or who amongst you is so abject that he will grovel in the squalid misery of his hut, or be content to be flung from the ditch side into the living tomb of the poorhouse, rather than charge proudly like brave men and free men, with that glorious young Meagher at their head, upon the hired mercenaries of their enemies? One bold, one decisive move.

One instant to take breath, and then a rising; a rush, a charge from north, south, east and west upon the English garrison, and *the land is ours.* Do your eyes flash, do your hearts throb at the prospect of having a *country?* For you have had no country. You have never felt the pride, the dignity, the majesty of independence. You could never lift up your head to heaven and glory in the name of Irishman for all Europe read the brand of *slave* upon your brow.

"Oh! that my words could burn like molten metal through your veins, and light up this ancient heroic daring which would make each man of you a Leonidas—each battlefield a Marathon— each pass a Thermopylæ. Courage! need I preach to Irishmen of courage? Is it so hard a thing then to die? Alas! do we not all die daily of broken hearts and shattered hopes, and tortures of mind and body that make life a weariness, and of weariness worse even than the tortures; for life is one long, slow agony of death.

"No! it cannot be death you fear; for you have braved the plague in the exile ship of the Atlantic, and plague in the exile's home beyond it; and famine and ruin, and a slave's life, and a dog's death; and hundreds, thousands, a *million* of you have

perished thus. Courage! You will not now belie
those old traditions of humanity that tell of this
divine God-gift within us. I have read of a Roman wife who stabbed herself before her husband's
eyes to teach him how to die. These million deaths
teach us as grand a lesson. To die for Ireland!
Yes; have we not sworn it in a thousand passionate
words by our poets and orators—in the grave resolves of councils, leagues and confederations. Now
is the moment to test whether you value most freedom or life. Now is the moment to strike, and by
striking save, and the day after the victory it will
be time enough to count your dead.

"But we do not provoke this war. History will
write of us—that Ireland endured wrongs unexam-
pled by any despotism—sufferings unequalled by
any people—her life-blood drained by a vampire
host of foreign masters and officials—her honour
insulted by a paid army of spies—her cries of despair stifled by the armed hand of legalised ruffian-
ism—that her peasants starved while they reaped
the corn for their foreign lords, because no man
gave them bread—that her pallid artisans pined
and wasted, because no man gave them work—that
her men of genius, the noblest and purest of her
sons, were dragged to a felon's cell, lest the people

might hear the voice of *truth,* and that in this horrible atrophy of all mental and physical powers, this stagnation of all existences, whoever dared to rise and demand wherefore it was that Ireland, made so beautiful by God, was made the plague spot of the universe by man—he was branded as a *felon*—imprisoned, robbed, tortured, chained, exiled, murdered. Thus history will write of us. And she will also write that Ireland did not start from this horrid trance of suffering and despair until 30,000 swords were at her heart, and even then she did not rise for vengeance, only *prepared to resist.* No—we are not the aggressors— we do not provoke this terrible war. Even with six million hearts to aid us, and with all the chance of success in our favour, we still offer terms to England. If she capitulates even now at the eleventh hour, and grants the moderate, the just demands of Ireland, our arms shall not be raised to sever the golden link that unites the two nations. And the chances of success *are* all with us. There is a Godlike strength in a just cause—a desperate energy in men who are fighting in their own land for the possession of that land—a glowing enthusiasm that scorns all danger when from success they can look onward to a future of unutterable glory and happiness for their country. Opposed to us are only a hired soldiery and a paid police who, mere trained machines even as they are, yet must shudder (for they are men) at the horrible task of butchery, under the blasphemed name of duty to which England summons them.   Brothers many of them are of this people they are called upon to murder—sons of the same soil—fellow-countrymen of those who are heroically struggling to elevate their common country.   Surely whatever humanity is left in them will shrink from being made the sad instruments of despotism and tyranny—they will blush to receive the purchase-money of England which hires them for the accursed and fratricidal work.   Would a Sicilian have been found in the ranks of Naples?   Would a Milanese have been detected in the fierce hordes of Austria?   No; for the Sicilians prize honour and the stately Milanese would strike the arm to the earth that would dare to offer them Austrian gold in payment for the blood of their own countrymen.   And heaven forbid that in *Ireland* could be found a band of armed fratricides to fight against their own land for the flag of a foreign tyrant.   But if indeed interest or coercion should tempt them into so horrible and unnatural a position, pity, a thousand times pity, for those brave officers who vaunt themselves on their honour. Pity for that brave soldiery whose Irish valour has made England illustrious that they must stain honour, and fame, and profession, and their brave swords by lending them to so infamous a cause. Ah! we need not tremble for a nation filled with a pure and holy enthusiasm, and fighting for all that human nature holds dear; but the masters of those hired mercenaries may well tremble for their cause, for the consciousness of eternal infamy will unnerve every arm that is raised to uphold it.

"If the government, then, do not come forward with honest, honourable and liberal concessions, let the war active and passive commence. *They* confide in the discipline of their troops—*we* in the righteousness of our cause. But not even a burning enthusiasm—which they have not—added to their discipline, could make a garrison of 30,000 men hold their ground against six millions. And one thing is certain—that if the people do not choose to fight the garrison, they may *starve* them. Adopt the Milan method—let no man sell to them. This passive warfare may be carried on in every village in Ireland, while more active hostilities are proceeding through all the large towns and cities. But, to gain possession of the capital should be the grand object of all their efforts. Let every line converge to this point. The Castle is the keystone of English power; take it, destroy it, burn it —at any hazard become masters of it, and on the same ground whence proceeded all those acts of insult and infamy which aroused the just retribution of a people's vengeance, establish a government in whom the people of all classes can place confidence.

"On this pedestal of fallen tyranny and corruption raise a structure of nobleness that will at once give security and prestige of time-honoured and trusted names to our revolution. For a people who rise to overthrow a despotism will establish no modification of it in its place. If they fight it is for absolute independence; and as the first step in a revolution should be to prevent the possibility of anarchy, the men elected to form this government ought at once to take the entire progress and organisation of the revolution under their protection and authority. It will be their duty to watch that no crime be suffered to stain the pure flag of Irish liberty. We must show to the world that we are fitted to govern ourselves; that we are, indeed, worthy to be a free nation, that the words union, liberty, country have as sacred a meaning in our hearts and actions as they are holy on our lips; that patriotism means not merely the wild irresistible force that crushed tyranny, but reconstruction, regeneration, heroism, sacrifice, sublimity; that we have not alone to break the fetters of Ireland, but to raise her to a glorious elevation—defend her, liberate her, ennoble her, sanctify her.

"Nothing is wanting now to complete our regeneration, to ensure our success, but to cast out those vices which have disgraced our name among the nations. There are terrible traditions shadowing the word *Liberty* in Ireland. Let it be our task, men of this generation—descendants of martyrs, and sufferers, and heroes, to make it a glad evangel of happiness—a reign of truth over fictions and symbols—of intellect over prejudice and conventionalism—of humanity over tyranny and oppression. Irishmen! this resurrection into a new life depends on you; for we have all lain dead. Hate, distrust, oppression, disunion, selfishness, bigotry—these things are Death. We must crush all vices—annihilate all evil passions—trample on them, as a triumphant Christ with his foot upon the serpent, and then the proud hallelujah of Freedom will rise to heaven from the lips of a pure, a virtuous, a regenerated, a God-blessed people; and this fair land of ours, which now affrights the world with its misery, will be one grand temple, in which we shall all kneel as brothers—one holy, peaceful, loving fraternity—sons of one common country—children of one God—heirs together of those blessings purchased by our blood—a heritage of freedom, justice, independence, prosperity and glory!"

CHAPTER II.

HOME, SCHOOL AND UNIVERSITY LIFE.

These were the distinguished parents of a son who attained still greater distinction, only to attract thereby the attention of the world to the family disgrace in the hour of his downfall. This was the bitterest drop in the cup of Oscar Wilde's sorrow. Writing from Reading Gaol soon after the death of his mother, he said (in "De Profundis") :

"No one knew how deeply I loved and honoured her. Her death was terrible to me; but I, once a lord of language, have no words in which to express my anguish and my shame. She and my father had bequeathed me a name they had made noble and honoured, not merely in literature, art, archæology, and science, but in the public history of my own country, in its evolution as a nation. I had disgraced that name eternally. I had made

it a low byword among low people. I had dragged
it through the very mire. I had given it to brutes
that they might make it brutal, and to foes that
they might turn it into a synonym for folly. What
I suffered then, and still suffer, is not for pen to
write, or paper to record. My wife, always kind
and gentle to me, rather than that I should hear
the news from indifferent lips, travelled, ill as she
was, all the way from Genoa to England to break to
me herself the tidings of so irreparable, so irre-
deemable, a loss."

Had Oscar Wilde known that he had also "given
his name" to *friends* "that they might make it"
the warrant of cruel and prejudged inquisition into
the character of these parents, in order, perchance,
to find some faint justification for the sin of their
son, then, indeed, would he have suffered the
crowning ecstasy of sorrow.

Miss Elgee married Dr. Wilde in Dublin in 1851.
The first child born to the Wildes was a son whom
they named William, after his father, but who was
always known as "Willy," a diminutive that is significant of a lovable nature, but when applied
throughout manhood is suggestive of weakness
and dependence.

Oscar, the second child, was born on the 16th of October, 1854, in the Wilde home at No. 1 Merrion Square, Dublin. As Mr. Sherard, his biographer, points out, this is a year or so earlier than is usually supposed, and than Wilde himself stated in the closing years of his life. "Wilde," says Sherard, "professed an adoration for youth; his works contain many almost rhapsodical eulogies of physical and mental immaturity; and no doubt that as he himself drew nearer to what he satirised in his plays as 'the usual age,' he gave as the year of his birth a date which made him appear two years younger than he really was. . . ."

A third child, a daughter, died in girlhood. Her memory was greatly revered by Oscar, who wrote what is probably the most exquisite of all his lyrics upon her early death:

REQUIESCAT.

Tread lightly, she is near
    Under the snow;
Speak gently, she can hear
    The daisies grow.

All her bright golden hair
  Tarnished with rust,
She that was young and fair
  Fallen to dust.

Lily-like, white as snow,
  She hardly knew
She was a woman, so
  Sweetly she grew.

Coffin-board, heavy stone,
  Lie on her breast;
I vex my heart alone,
  She is at rest.

Peace, peace, she cannot hear
  Lyre or sonnet;
All my life's buried here,
  Heap earth upon it.

A deep affection existed in childhood between
"Willy" and Oscar, persisting, indeed, through an
estrangement that developed in later years from
circumstances which do not enter into the scope
of this memoir. Mr. Sherard in his "Life of Oscar Wilde" reports an incident related by Oscar

that charmingly illustrates the love he bore to his brother:

"I had a toy bear of which I was very fond indeed, so fond that I used to take it to bed with me, and I thought that nothing could make me more unhappy than to lose my bear. Well, one day Willy asked me for it; and I was so fond of Willy that I gave it to Willy, I remember, without a pang. Afterward, however, the enormity of the sacrifice I had made impressed itself upon me. I considered that such an act merited the greatest gratitude and love in return, and whenever Willy crossed me in any way I used to say: 'Willy, you don't deserve my bear. Give me back my bear.' And for years afterwards, after we had grown up, whenever we had a slight quarrel, I used to say the same: 'Willy, you don't deserve my bear. You must give me back my bear.'"

Until he was eleven years old Oscar Wilde received his education at home. He had private tutors, but perhaps his best tutors were his father and mother. His mother, with her poetical endowments, probably influenced him more than the father. Sir William Wilde was a great admirer of the beauties of nature, and sought to impress his worship upon the rapidly maturing mind of his young son. But in later life Oscar indicates that his father's enthusiasms were by no means shared by him. He was wont to describe the country as "rather tedious," and vastly preferred life in the cities. "One can only write in cities," he wrote to a friend; and goes on to speak of "the splendid whirl and swirl of life in London." The simple life was not for him. In the first essay in "Intentions" he makes Vivian, his mouthpiece, say:

"*Vivian*—Enjoy Nature! I am glad to say that I have entirely lost that faculty. People tell us that Art makes us love Nature more than we loved her before; that it reveals her secrets to us; and that after a careful study of Corot and Constable we see things in her that had escaped our observation. My own experience is that the more we study Art, the less we care for Nature. What Art really reveals to us is Nature's lack of design, her curious crudities, her extraordinary monotony, her absolutely unfinished condition. Nature has good intentions, of course, but, as Aristotle once said, she cannot carry them out. When I look at a land-

scape I cannot help seeing all its defects. It is
fortunate for us, however, that Nature is so imper-
fect, as otherwise we should have had no Art at
all.   Art is our spirited protest, our gallant attempt to teach Nature her proper place. As for
the infinite variety of Nature, that is a pure
myth. . . ."

And shortly afterwards Vivian goes on to say:

"But Nature is so uncomfortable. Grass is hard
and lumpy and damp, and full of dreadful black
insects. Why, even Morris's poorest workman could
make you a more comfortable seat than the whole
of Nature can. . . .   If Nature had been comfortable mankind would never have invented architecture, and I prefer houses to the open air. In a
house we all feel of the proper proportions. Everything is subordinated to us, fashioned for our use
and our pleasure. Egotism itself, which is indoor
life."

Oscar Wilde was brought up amid luxurious surroundings. His father's house, No. 1 Merrion
Square, Dublin, is still among the handsomest
houses of that city. The father was a high liver

and extremely hospitable; the mother was fond of entertaining literary people, artists, clever bohemians. So the young Oscar came in contact in his own home with a great variety of people. In his early years he already gave proof of great cleverness. When he was nine years of age Lady Wilde said to a caller: "Willy is all right, but Oscar is wonderful, wonderful. He can do anything."

Oscar Wilde seems always to have felt that he might have done "anything." He was over-conscious of great powers, and haunted by a feeling that he had not properly utilised them.

The following passage is taken from a biographical notice of Oscar Wilde which appeared in 1891, and which thus refers to his early education:

"The son of two remarkable people, Mr. Wilde had a remarkable upbringing. From his earliest childhood his principal companions were his father and mother and their friends. Now wandering about Ireland with the former in quest of archæological treasures, now listening in Lady Wilde's *salon* to the wit and thought of Ireland, the boy, before his eighth year had learnt the ways to 'the shores of old romance,' had seen all the apples

plucked from the tree of knowledge, and had gazed
with wondering eyes into 'the younger day.' This
upbringing suited his idiosyncrasy; indeed, with
his temperament it is impossible to conceive what
else could have been done with him. He had, of
course, tutors, and the run of a library contain-
ing the best literature, and went to a Royal school;
but it was at his father's dinner-table and in his
mother's drawing-room that the best of his early
education was obtained. Another experience, unusual to boyhood, had a powerful formative influence. He travelled much in France and Germany,
becoming acquainted with the works of Heine and
Goethe, but more especially with French literature
and the French temperament. It was in France,
at an age when other boys are grinding at grammar
or cricket, that Oscar Wilde began to realise in
some measure what he was. There he found himself for the first time in a wholly congenial environment. The English temperament—there are
those who deny that such a thing exists—'like
sweet bells jangled, out of tune and harsh,' responds
indifferently to the æsthetic. In France Mr. Wilde
found everywhere exquisite susceptibility to beauty,
and found also that he himself, an Irish Celt, possessed this susceptibility in all its intensity. French

and Greek literature were the two earliest passions
of his artistic life."

At the age of eleven Oscar was sent to Portora
Royal School, Enniskillen, which is under the gov-
ernment of the Fermanagh Protestant Board of
Education, and is mainly a training-school for the
universities, and especially for Trinity College,
Dublin, where young Wilde later matriculated.

At Portora he made rapid progress in the clas-
sics, but found himself very backward in mathe-
matics. He had no head for figures, and they remained throughout his life more or less a mystery
to him. This may more or less explain his wild
extravagances in money matters, for the faculty
of calculation seems to be lacking in the mental
make-up of most spendthrifts. His biographer,
Sherard, thus tells of Wilde's schooldays at Portora:

"Oscar Wilde was a big boy, very tall for his
age, and distinctly heavy of build. One of his
schoolfellows says that 'he used to flop about pon-
derously.' He was not popular with the other
boys. For one thing, he never played any games.
In later life he used to say that he objected to

cricket because the attitudes assumed were so inde-
cent. He never rowed on the lake; and he had for
the musketry instructor and the drill sergeant con-
tempt mingled with pity. His manner was very
reserved, and he used to keep aloof from the other
boys. Another characteristic which made for his
unpopularity amongst his schoolfellows, just as in
later life it raised up against him so many implac-
able enemies, was the extraordinary gift he had of
saying trenchant things about others. He was
a very clever boy at giving nicknames. He was
the ironical sponsor to the whole school, from
the Rev. William Steele, D.D., the headmaster,
down to the smallest boy in class 1B. As a
man, few wits have ever said cleverer and at the
same time more biting things about their contemporaries. This capacity of his and his ruthless
exercise thereof account for much of the hatred
that is still alive against him years after his lonely
death. Of one very famous contemporary Irish
writer he remarked: 'He has no enemies, but he is
intensely disliked by his friends.' Of the son of
a famous pianist he once said, when the fact of
this parentage was stated to him: 'Well, I am glad
that he has managed to survive it.'

"Already in those days young Oscar Wilde showed that fondness for distinguished attire which ever marked him in life. He is remembered at Portora as the only boy there who used to wear a top hat. 'It was always a very fashionable hat, of the latest style.' All the boys at Portora were provided, by school regulations as to the outfit, with one black silk hat, but this was for Sunday wear only. Oscar never discarded his. He was always very well dressed, and wore his hair long. 'He had a good wisp of hair!' is said of him still in Enniskillen. He did not appear to be very friendly with his brother Willy. 'He was very superior in his manner towards Willy.' The latter was much more popular with the boys. The little boys at Portora, especially, had the greatest affection for Willy Wilde. Even in those early days he had all the charming *talents de société* which afterwards won him much success. He used to tell stories to the children, and he used to play the piano for them.

"Oscar was considered exceedingly clever in literature—that is to say, in his knowledge of books. At the same time the future author of 'Intentions' never showed any superiority in composition. 'He never stood out in essays,' remarks one of his masters, who adds: 'Oscar Wilde was never looked upon as a formidable competitor by the boys who went in for examinations in Portora school.' His conduct was uniformly good. There was not a breath of a complaint about him in any way, except some short time before he left the school, when, as one of his schoolfellows relates, 'he got into an awful row with the headmaster. He had cheeked old Steele something awful.' That there was nothing of the decadent about Oscar Wilde in his school-days is the unanimous declaration of many men who were boys at school with him. He was a great reader, and assimilated what he read in a remarkable manner. He used to get through a book with a speed that astonished everybody; and what he had read thus rapidly, he used to remember. He read nothing but English books, and these were generally classical novels. He displayed no particular efficiency in French in those days. He had a great fondness for handsome books and choice editions. 'When he came so prominently before the world as an æsthete,' relates a Don at T. C. D., 'we all tried to remember any indication that he had given as a lad of a taste for beautiful things, and the only thing that we would recall in this connection was that he always had most expensive copies of class-books. He had, for instance, a beautiful large paper edition of Æschylus.' During his last year at Portora, when he was a lad of sixteen, his eager thirst for knowledge and his great receptivity were matters of observation and comment. Often when Mr. Purser was instructing the class in history or in geography Oscar Wilde would contrive by means of some cleverly put question to lead the master into a disquisition on some topic on which he desired to gain information. The subject in hand would be forgotten; the master, ever prompted by his pupil, would unbosom himself of his store of learning. Sometimes the whole of the hour would be thus absorbed. At other times the master would bring the discussion back to the subject of the lesson, and then it was a sight to see the lad, all alert, thinking and planning how, next day, he could turn the master once more on to the question in which he needed instruction—questions often as abstruse as the relative definitions of nominalism and realism."

At the age of seventeen, in October of 1871, Oscar Wilde matriculated at Trinity College, Dublin, and obtained second place in the matriculation examination. He remained at Trinity only a year, but left behind him an excellent reputation for scholarship and for general deportment. "He left this college," said one of the Dons, "with the very highest character." He won a scholarship and also the Berkeley Gold Medal, a distinction which is highly prized at Trinity. This medal was founded by the famous Bishop Berkeley, the eminent philosopher. The subject in which candidates were examined in the year that Wilde took the prize was "The Fragments of the Greek Comic Poets, as edited by Meincke."

During the following year Wilde entered Oxford, matriculating at Magdalen College, and winning a demyship of the annual value of £95.

In "De Profundis" he writes: "I want to get to the point when I shall be able to say quite simply, and without affectation, that the two great turning-points in my life were when my father sent me to Oxford, and when society sent me to prison."

During Wilde's first term at Oxford he fell for a short time under the influence of John Ruskin, who was lecturing twice a week on the "Æsthetic and Mathematical Schools of Art in Florence." Mr. Sherard rather scouts the idea that his attendance upon these lectures had any very lasting effect or permanent influence upon Oscar Wilde's mental outlook. He says:

"Oscar Wilde was a constant attendant at these lectures, and there can be no doubt that they produced a very strong impression on his mind, as, indeed, Ruskin's discourses did on every man who heard them. They must have opened up a new field of interest to the young Irishman, have afforded him new subjects on which to talk, and have suggested to him, by the spectacle of the great enthusiasm which Mr. Ruskin aroused, the opportunism of a minor apostolate in a creed so obviously popular and successful. But there do not appear to be any grounds for saying, as has so often been said, that Oscar Wilde was greatly influenced by Mr. Ruskin. It was not probable that this would be so, seeing that the whole period of Ruskin's public appearances that term did not exceed twenty-four days, and that in that period it is not possible for one man to influence another to the extent of tingeing his whole psychology. Oscar Wilde was a man of extraordinary receptivity, but even to him it would have been impossible to absorb Ruskin's teachings and example so that these should have any permanent effect on his character in so short a period. At that time he was fresh at Oxford; a hundred things presented themselves every day to divert his attention; his mentality was in no way prepared to receive the master's teachings; and altogether it seems as absurd to state that Ruskin influenced the whole of his character and his life by means of the eight lectures which Oscar Wilde attended as a freshman during his first term in Oxford, as it was incredible that the perusal of a single book could pervert the mental composition of a man. These matters have to be looked at from a scientific point of view; the plain facts have to be considered and the evidence that can be adduced. There is no trace of any Ruskin influence in Oscar Wilde's after-life, and it would be a psychological miracle if there had been."

But though Ruskin may have left no lasting impression upon the mind of Wilde, he certainly appears to have influenced him strongly during his Oxford life and perhaps later, for it seems as if Ruskin had turned Wilde's mind towards æsthetics and æstheticism, and so, perhaps, was in a measure responsible for the affected rôle of an apostle of æstheticism which it pleased Wilde to play for some time after his graduation from Oxford. In his "The Æsthetic Movement in England," Mr. Walter Hamilton, in a chapter treating of Oscar Wilde, says of the latter's Oxford life:

"Unfortunately, Mr. Ruskin left for Venice at the end of Mr. Wilde's first term; not, however, before he had inoculated a number of the young collegians with artistic tastes. Mr. Wilde occupied some fine old wainscoted rooms over the river in that college which is thought by many to be the most beautiful in Oxford. These rooms he had decorated with painted ceilings and handsome dados, and they were filled with treasures of art picked up at home and abroad; and here he held social meetings, which were attended by numbers of the men who were interested in art, or music, or poetry, and who for the most part practised some one of these in addition to the ordinary collegiate studies."

And Mr. Hamilton also quotes the following passage by "one who was acquainted with Mr. Wilde at Oxford":

"He soon began to show his taste for art and china, and before he had been at Oxford very long his rooms were quite the show ones of the college and of the university, too. He was fortunate enough to obtain the best-situated rooms in the college, on what is called the kitchen staircase, having a lovely view over the river Cherwell and the beautiful Magdalen walks and Magdalen bridge. His rooms were three in number, and the walls were entirely panelled. The two sitting-rooms were connected by an arch, where folding doors had at one time stood. His blue china was supposed by *connoisseurs* to be very valuable and fine, and there was plenty of it. The panelled walls were thickly hung with old engravings—chiefly engravings of the fair sex artistically clad as nature clad them. He was hospitable, and on Sunday nights after 'Common Room' his rooms were generally the scene of conviviality, where undergraduates of all descriptions and tastes were to be met, drinking punch, or a 'B. and S.,' with their cigars. It was at one of these entertainments that he made his well-known remark, 'Oh, would that I could live up to my blue china!' His chief amusement was riding, though he never used to hunt. He was generally to be met on the cricket-field, but never played himself; and he was a regular attendant at his college barge to see the May eight-oar races, but he never used to trust his massive form to a boat himself."

Indeed, at this time appears to be the beginning

of Oscar Wilde's affected pose, which seems to have been keenly resented by some of his fellow students, who gave vent to their displeasure by waylaying the "blue china cove" while he was out for a walk. They bound him with cords and dragged him to the top of a hill. Although hurt and bruised, the victim did not protest, and when he was at length released he flicked the dust from his coat and re-marked as he examined the prospect: "Yes, the view from this hill is really very charming."

. While he was at Oxford, Wilde contributed a number of poems and prose writings to Dublin magazines. One of his earliest published prose writings, descriptive of the grave of Keats, was contributed to the *Irish Monthly,* and was written in Rome in 1877. It was concluded by the poem on Keats here entitled "Heu Miserandi Puer."

During the Oxford days, in 1877, Wilde made a journey to Greece, together with a party which accompanied John Pentland Mahaffy, and this brought a new and determinative influence into his life; it was a confirmation of his dreams and visions of beauty undreamed, of "the light that never was on sea or land." In his own words, in regard to this experience, "the worship of sorrow gave place again to the worship of beauty." For

Wilde had been coquetting with Roman Catholicism through his inclination for the spiritual element in art, and while in this frame of mind had written his notable poem, "Rome Unvisited," which won high praise from Cardinal Newman. This journey, it has been said, contributed to make a "healthy Pagan" of the man who was hesitating whether to join the Church of Rome. Wilde himself declared that the lesson he learned from his travel in Greece was that it was very right for the Greek gods to be in the Vatican. "Helen," he affirmed, "took precedence of the *Mater Dolorosa.*"

Wilde was so taken up with the delights of his tour in Greece that he overstayed his time, and upon returning to Oxford was fined for not having made his appearance at the college at the time required of him. The fine, £45, was, however, returned to him during the following year, when he won great distinction by taking a First Class in the "Honour Finals," and by winning the Newdigate Prize for English Verse. The topic for this Newdigate competition was Ravenna, which, happily, he had recently visited, and had already in his mind an idea for a poem on this subject. "Ravenna" exhibits a distinct advance on any of his previous work, and contains many beautiful lines. Altogether, Wilde acquitted himself very ably in his classes at Oxford and left behind him a distinguished reputation for scholarship and literary ability.

CHAPTER III.

EARLY LONDON LIFE.

In the spring of 1878 Wilde took up his residence in London, living for some months in a couple of furnished rooms in Salisbury Street, off the Strand. Later he moved to Charles Street, Grosvenor Square, and these lodgings he retained until his marriage.

He had evidently made up his mind to make himself known, to win some kind of fame, and direct attention to himself as quickly as possible.

So he soon began to attract attention by his eccentricities. He frequented the drawing-rooms of Madame Modjeska and Mrs. Langtry, for both of whom he expressed the wildest devotion. Mrs. Langtry was first both pleased and amused by Wilde's adoration, but when his rhapsodies and dreams failed to divert her, she was seen less frequently at his rose-colored afternoon teas; one peculiarity of which, borrowed from his mother, was the drawn blinds and the dim, mysterious light, which made it almost impossible for fellow guests to recognise one another. Once a stranger at these assemblies asked in an awed whisper which was Mrs. Langtry. Wilde overheard him. "What an absurd question!" he cried. "If the sun shone, I should know it was the sun!"

Sandwiched between "the sun that shone" and "the haunting eyes of Modjeska" was the great Bernhardt, whom Wilde began to cultivate as soon as she established herself at her house in Prince's Gate. He had a mania for distinguished foreigners. He acted as interpreter between Henry Irving and Bastien Le Page when the latter was painting the actor's portrait. He amused all London by the famous description of Irving's legs— "One is a poem and the other is a symphony."

It was at this period that Wilde developed his affectation in dress. He clad himself in black velvet, with knickerbockers and black silk stockings. He sported a Byronic collar. He wore his hair long. He carried a lily in his hand even on the streets. And at the most stifling receptions he would not doff his fur-lined overcoat.

Du Maurier got hold of him and caricatured him

as Postlewaite in *Punch,* and Burnand reproduced
him in his satiric comedy, "Where's the Cat?" Gilbert also satirized Wilde as Bunthorne in "Patience." The ridicule of the stage frightened
many of Wilde's disciples into donning everyday
garments and giving up their æsthetic fads, but
Wilde, undaunted, would not yield to popular ridicule. Even at a supper party at which the present
King Edward, then the Prince of Wales, was a
guest, Wilde clung to his characteristic costume.
It happened that Grossmith, the original Bunthorne, was also present. He yielded to the general importunity to sing the famous Bunthorne
solo. The presence of the original "Pure Young
Man" gave additional zest to the verses. At their
close Wilde was dragged bodily up before His
Royal Highness, with the words, "This is the
man." But he imperturbably preserved his placid
smile amid the general merriment.

It is a pity that Wilde began his career by making himself a "motley to the view," for the jingle
of his jester's bells echoed about him for a long
time, and the public would not take him seriously
long after the cap and bells had been discarded.
Dr. Holmes, however, has said that every successful man must have something of the charlatan

in him, and there was method in Wilde's postures. The notoriety he acquired enabled him to secure a publisher for his first volume of verse, and later won him an invitation to lecture in America.

Some verses which appeared in the London *World* sound the dominant note of public opinion during the heyday of Wilde's career as the apostle of the Æsthetic Movement. They were labeled "Ego up to Snuffibus Poeta."

"Albeit nurtured in democracy
    And liking best that state Bohemian
    Where each man borrows sixpence and no man
Has aught but paper collars; yet I see
Exactly where to take a liberty.
    Better to be thought one, whom most abuse
    For speech of donkey and for look of goose,
Than that the world should pass in silence by.
    Wherefore I wear a sunflower in my coat,
Cover my shoulders with my flowing hair,
    Tie verdant satin round my open throat,
Culture and love I cry, and ladies smile,
And seedy critics overflow with bile,
While with my Prince long Sykes's meal I share."

But many discerning ones in London at this

time saw behind Wilde's mask of affectation and discerned his real cleverness. A noble English lady, who met him in his early London days, subsequently wrote of him: "I thought I had never met so wonderful and brilliant a creature."

Julian Hawthorne, who made Wilde's acquaintance at this time, writes:

"It was when he was fresh to London, in 1879, that my acquaintance with him began. We had several acquaintances in common, and I saw him frequently. I was impressed, like others, with the brilliance of his mental quality; his repartee, persiflage, paradox, and society small talk in general were extraordinary. At the same time it was obvious enough that he was 'playing' society for all there was in it; he despised it, made game of it, and at every point kept his personal profit and advantage in view. A tone of half cynical, half good-natured mockery was his habitual wear in society; while at the same time he professed extravagant ideals in the line of æstheticism and the conduct of life. Something in him repelled and something attracted me in him; but it seemed to me that he was making a gratuitous error in aiming to succeed in the world by humbugging it; he was strong enough to be sincere. One night when we were walking homeward along a deserted London street I put this to him frankly; there were no witnesses, why would he not, for once, speak out frankly in real tones? But he would not. 'The one thing about me that nobody seems to understand is,' he declared, 'that I am always absolutely sincere.' "

At the height of the ridicule that was poured upon him by the general public Wilde's first book of poems appeared. It was well received by the public, but not by the critics. The volume was made up mainly of reprints of poems which Wilde had contributed to various periodicals and journals in Dublin and London. Four editions were sold within a few weeks, and the popularity of the volume is not to be wondered at, for it contained such poems as "Ave Imperatrix," "The Garden of Eros," "Hélas!" and the neo-Catholic poems, sufficient indeed to give evidence that a true poet had come into his own.

But by the critics, who probably at that time could hardly take Wilde seriously, the volume was by no means well received. The *Saturday Review* disposed of it briefly and somewhat contemptuously, thus: "Mr. Wilde's verses belong to a class which is the special terror of the reviewers, the poetry which is neither good nor bad, which calls for neither praise nor ridicule, and in which we search in vain for any personal touch of thought or music." Lower down: "The great fault of all such writing as this is the want of literary sincerity which it displays. For instance, Mr. Wilde brings into his verse the names of innumerable birds and flowers, because he likes the sound of their names, not because he has made any observation of their habits. He thinks that the meadow-sweet and the wood-anemone bloom at the same time, that that shy and isolated flower, the hare-bell, 'breaks across the woodlands in masses,' 'like a sudden flush of sea,' and that owls are commonly met with in mid-ocean." Strong exception is next taken to the sensual tone of the poems, and the review concludes with the following sentence: "This book is not without traces of cleverness, but it is marred everywhere by imitation, insincerity, and bad taste."

The *Athenæum*, for July 23, 1881, came out on its first page with a long review of Wilde's poems, but it was, on the whole, an unfavorable one. It runs as follows:

"Mr. Wilde's volume of poems may be regarded as the evangel of a new creed. From other gospels it differs in coming after, instead of before, the cult it seeks to establish. It has thus the advantage of answering objections as well as propounding dogma, and its rebuke of irreverence, instead of being vague and discursive, is exact and to the point. One drawback from these advantages is that what should be promulgation of truth takes occasionally a form that might be mistaken for apology, and that querulous protest disappoints at times those who anticipate a clarion note of defiance, that the mind of the poet has been vexed and the soul of the teacher troubled by "shallow wit" is obvious. In one of these poems of fourteen lines which find occasional acceptance as sonnets, Mr. Wilde declares:

"This mighty empire hath but feet of clay:
     Of all its ancient chivalry and might
     Our little island is forsaken quite:
Some enemy hath stolen its crown of bay,
And from its hills that voice hath passed away
     Which spake of freedom: O come out of it,
     Come out of it, my soul, thou art not fit
For this vile traffic-house, where day by day

Wisdom and reverence are sold at mart,
   And the rude people rage with ignorant cries
   Against an heritage of centuries.
It mars my calm: wherefore in dreams of art
And loftiest culture I would stand apart,
   Neither for God, nor for His enemies.'

"The kind of neutrality indicated in the last line of this poem corresponds with and recalls that invoked by the hero of a Western adventure with a 'grizzly,' who, without asking any direct aid from the superior powers, urged them at least not to 'side with the b'ar.'

"In the 'Garden of Eros' the doctrine of the new worship is promulgated intelligibly, if not very musically:

'Spirit of Beauty! tarry still a while,
   They are not dead, thine ancient votaries,
Some few there are to whom thy radiant smile
   Is better than a thousand victories,
Though all the nobly slain of Waterloo
Rise up in wrath against them! tarry still, there
      are a few
Who for thy sake would give their manhood
   And consecrate their being. I, at least,

Have done so, made thy lips my daily food,
   And in thy temples found a goodlier feast
Than this starved age can give me, spite of all
Its new-found creeds so sceptical and so dog-
      matical.'

"This, at least, is challenge. It is a little difficult to know what the 'slain of Waterloo' have to
do in the matter, or why their phantoms should
rise in wrath to combat with the ancient votaries
of the Spirit of Beauty, who are not yet dead.
Since the days of Macbeth a state of affairs which
the Thane understood to have existed before his
time, that

'When the brains were out the man would die,'

has returned, and the slain of Waterloo, or those
of them buried in England, will scarcely hear the
'pother o'er their heads' created by modern æstheticism. 'Victories' is a singularly bad rhyme to
'votaries,' and the last line of the quotation affords
a notable instance of bathos. Still, if the verses
have not much poetry, they at least show courage.
In a sonnet entitled 'Tædium Vitæ,' the protest
seems most directly personal:

'To stab my youth with desperate knives, to wear
   This paltry age's gaudy livery,
To let each base hand filch my treasury,
   To mesh my soul within a woman's hair,
And be mere Fortune's lackeyed groom—I swear
   I love it not! these things are less to me
Than the thin foam that frets upon the sea,
   Less than the thistle-down of summer air
Which hath no seed: better to stand aloof
   Far from these slanderous fools who mock my
         life
Knowing me not, better the lowliest roof
   Fit for the meanest hind to sojourn in,
Than to go back to that hoarse cave of strife
   Where my white soul first kissed the mouth
         of sin.'

"Worship of beauty, whatever shape it may take,
is not likely to be a thing of which to be ashamed,
and those by whom it is derided may well be
chargeable with offences far more mischievous than
a little false æstheticism.   We fail to see, however,
that the apostle of the new worship has any distinct message.   With Wordsworth, and with some
other men, Mr. Wilde holds we should be better
for the return of Milton.   With the Laureate as

with Wordsworth, he disapproves strongly of the
commercial tendencies of the age. With others besides poets he does not quite know what to make
of modern demagogism, with some aspects of which
he sympathises, while others are wholly repellant
to him; and he is greatly exercised by the position
of the Pope at Rome.

"It is doubtful, however, how far familiarity
with the nudities of passion will go towards setting the world straight. A study so clever as
'Manon Lescaut' has not done much to check the
movement towards feminine suffrage. We doubt,
then, whether any number of rhapsodies like 'Char-
mides' will serve a purpose such as Mr. Wilde
seems to desire when he sighs for a return to
Milton.

"Turning to the execution of the poems, there is
something to admire. Mr. Wilde has a keen perception of certain aspects of natural beauty. Single lines might be extracted which convey striking
and accurate pictures. The worst faults are artificiality and insincerity, and an extravagant ac-
centuation of whatever in modern verse most closely approaches the *estilo culto* of the sixteenth century. Imitation of previous writers goes far enough
seriously to damage the claim to originality, and

Portora Royal School, Enniskillen, where Oscar Wilde received his early education.

Page 64

the workmanship is slovenly in the sense that those
half rhymes which in pre-Tennysonian days were
tolerated in the writings of the best poets are employed with a freedom that deprives the task of
writing verse of the greater portion of its diffi-
culty. . . . In dealing, meanwhile, with imitation,
we pass over the use, in two consecutive lines, of
such epithets, directly taken from Milton, as
'swinked' shepherd and 'wattled' sheep-'cotes.' Does
Mr. Wilde suppose he could ever have written the
verses in 'Ave Imperatrix' commencing:

'But the sad dove, that sits alone
   In England—she hath no delight.

'In vain the laughing girl will lean
   To greet her love with love-lit eyes;
Down in some treacherous black ravine,
   Clutching his flag, the dead boy lies,'

if the Laureate had not given us the noble picture
in 'In Memoriam,'

'Oh somewhere, meek, unconscious dove,' etc. ?

"The sonnet on the 'Massacres of the Christians

in Bulgaria' reflects Milton's sonnet on the 'Massacres in Piedmont.'   The 'Garden of Eros' recalls
at times Mr. Swinburne—at times Alexander
Smith.   In the descriptions of flowers which occur
in the poem last named there is a direct and reiterated imitation of Shakespeare.

> 'Some violets lie
> That will not look the gold sun in the face
> For fear of too much splendour'—

reminds one of the

> 'Pale primroses
> That die unmarried ere they can behold
> Bright Phœbus in his strength.'

Mr. Wilde's

> 'Budding marjoram, which but to kiss
> Would sweeten Cytheræa's lips'

and his

> 'Meadow-sweet
> Whiter than Juno's throat'

bring back the

> 'Violets dim,
> But sweeter than the lids of Juno's eyes
> Or Cytheræa's breath.'

And the 'rustling bluebells'—rustling bluebells is a vile phrase—that come

> 'Almost before the blackbird finds a mate,
> And overstay the swallow'

are but the daffodils

> 'That come before the swallow dares.'

"Traces of this kind of imitation abound, and there is scarcely a poet of high mark in the present century whose influence is not perceptible.

"What, however, impresses most unfavourably the reader is the over-indulgence in metaphor, in affected neologisms, and in conceits behind which sense and reason are obscured. Gradually during recent years this style has grown upon us, until the poetic literature of the latter half of the nineteenth century seems likely to be classed with that produced by Lyly and the Euphuists. Of whatever is most vicious in a style which grows out of a misunderstanding worship of Keats, Mr. Wilde supplies abundant illustrations, and the whole is as inflated and insincere as it can well be. Work of this nature has no element of endurance, and Mr. Wilde's poems, in spite of some grace and beauty, as we have said, will, when their temporary notoriety is exhausted, find a place on the shelves of those only who hunt after the curious in literature. They may perhaps serve as an illustration in some chapter on the revival in the nineteenth century of the Gorgonism of the sixteenth."

Other reviews were equally unfavorable. The time had not yet come for taking Oscar Wilde seriously as a serious author. The babel of the comic press, which had poured a perfect storm of ridicule upon Wilde, undoubtedly had made itself felt. *Punch,* in reviewing the book, said:

"The cover is consummate, the paper is distinctly precious, the binding is beautiful, and the type is utterly too. 'Poems,' by Oscar Wilde, that is the title of the book of the æsthetic singer, which comes to us arrayed in white vellum and gold.

There is a certain amount of originality about the binding, but that is more than can be said for the inside of the volume. Mr. Wilde may be æsthetic, but he is not original. This is a volume of echoes, it is Swinburne and water, while here and there we notice that the author has been reminiscent of Mr. Rossetti and Mrs. Browning."

Again the charge of imitation; but what poet, especially what young poet, is not imitative? The music of the "grand old masters" naturally wakes echoes. Some one has sagely remarked that the poets are a long procession of gentlemen with their hands in each other's pockets. It is strange that some of the reviewers of the time did not discover that despite occasional imitation there was also great originality in these poems, and that certainly as the first offerings of a young poet they gave the very greatest promise for the future.

The "Poems" attracted wide attention in America, and had a considerable sale here, so that when he came to this country on a lecture tour he was known as a poet as well as the leader of the "Æsthetic Movement and School," but it was the latter character that excited curiosity here and brought throngs to hear him.

He sailed for New York on December 24, 1881, and during an extended tour delivered his lectures on "The English Renaissance" and "The Decorative Arts," besides other more informal talks. Here, as in England, it was the outward Oscar Wilde that attracted attention, his peculiar dress, his exaggerated manner, his reported devotion to sunflower and lily, but the real man behind these affectations left a deep impress upon the country. Many who came to scoff at his lectures in a certain sense remained to pray.

By the public press throughout the country Wilde was ridiculed, satirized, and caricatured, and although, as one of his friends records, he suffered poignantly from these attacks, still he undoubtedly occasionally provoked them, and, mayhap, deliberately. His remark in an interview upon arriving in New York, "I am not exactly pleased with the Atlantic. It is not so majestic as I expected," occasioned an infinite amount of humorous comment and satirical verses, as did later also his oft-quoted remark about the Falls of Niagara: "I was disappointed with Niagara. Most people must be disappointed with Niagara. Every American bride is taken there, and the sight of the stupendous waterfall must be one of the earliest if not the keenest disappointments in American married life."

Amid such a storm of ridicule, largely echoed from across the water, it is no wonder that it was some time before Wilde's lectures won the appreciation that they deserved. His audiences mostly came to be amused, not to listen, and the critics appear to have attended in the same spirit, with an occasional exception, though almost apologetically the *Sun* remarked of the lecture on "The English Renaissance," "It is not a performance so trifling as to insult the intelligence of the audience, but a carefully prepared essay which proves its author to be a man of cultivation, taste, imagination, and refinement."

The estimates of these lectures have undergone a transformation since the day in which they were delivered, and their saneness and brilliancy, as well as the influence they left behind them, are now recognized.

"As a plea for the encouragement of the handi-craftsman," writes Mr. Glaenzer in regard to the lecture on "Decorative Arts," "for the rejection of the hideously naturalistic tendency in house furnishing; for the establishment of museums, enriched by the finest examples from the finest periods of decorative art; for beautiful surroundings for children, and for schools in which these children might develop their artistic proclivities under the guidance of artists and capable artisans—as a *plea* for all that is beautiful, noble, and sane in art, this lecture falls little short of being a masterpiece."

Oscar Wilde's lecture tour in America will be treated in the succeeding chapter by a man who is, of all men, the most competent to do it, Col. W. F. Morse, who managed the lecture tours, both here and in England. Brought as he was in such close touch with Wilde, Colonel Morse's reminiscences have a peculiar interest, and throw illuminating side lights upon the character and personality of Oscar Wilde.

CHAPTER IV.

AMERICAN LECTURES.

By W. F. Morse.

No sketch of Oscar Wilde would be complete without some account of his career before the lecture audiences and public of the American cities, an episode in his life that did much for the man himself and at the time was a large factor for awakening and stimulating the sense and appreciation of what is true and what false in household art and decoration as applied to the homes and surroundings of the people.

It was the writer's work for a period of nearly a year to be responsible for the public appearance of Mr. Wilde before the American and Canadian public, in the way of preparation for his coming.

Gilbert & Sullivan's opera "Patience" was produced at the Standard Theatre, Broadway, New

York, Mr. Wm. Henderson, manager, on the 22d
of September, 1881, by Mr. R. D'Oyley Carte, then
proprietor of the Savoy Theatre, London, and manager throughout the world for the operas of the
famous collaborators in this domain of satirical
and musical comedy. "Pinafore" had made them
known, "The Pirates of Penzance" increased their
popularity. "Patience," with its central figure of
the Æsthetic Apostle, was the latest expression of
a new cult, of which we in America had somewhat
vague impressions through the Philistinic press.

The instantaneous hit and continued success of
the opera in New York indicated that the public
would be still further interested in the personnel of
the man who was said to be the leading light of the
new gospel of art, and the time was opportune.

The lecture tour of Mr. Archibald Forbes, the
famous war correspondent, who, under the management of Mr. Carte and the writer, had just concluded a successful five-months' tour in this country, and was then preparing for a final trip to
the Pacific Coast and a voyage to Australia, was
taken as a good omen for the success of another
English lecturer.

One afternoon in September, 1881, a lady—well
known in English and American newspaper cir-

cles as a writer upon the current society topics of the day on both sides of the water—suggested that perhaps Mr. Wilde would consent to give a series of lectures in this country. At once a cable was sent:

NEW YORK, Sept. 30, '81.

OSCAR WILDE, 1 Ovington Square, London.

Responsible agent asks me to enquire if you will consider offer he makes by letter for fifty readings, beginning November first. This is confidential. Answer.   ————.

The reply came promptly:

LONDON, Oct. 1, 1881.

Yes, if offer good.   WILDE.

Chelsea, Tite Street.

Within a short time after the receipt of the letter concluding final details of business arrangements proposed, Mr. Wilde cabled he would leave by the steamer Arizona, December 24, 1881. All details of Mr. Wilde's first appearance were left in my hands, I then being associated with Mr. Carte, as business manager, in New York. There were prepared a short biographical sketch of Mr. Wilde's parents, his upbringing, his school and college training, his preparation for serious literary work, some quotations from his volume of poems, his identification with the æsthetic movement in England, and the merest hint or indication as to the mode or method by which Mr. Wilde would express his views upon the subject announced for his first address, "The English Renaissance."

Upon his arrival, January 2, 1882, he was met by the usual interviewers at quarantine, to whom he frankly gave some idea of the purposes of his visit. This was distorted and twisted in a way intended to provoke ridicule, and "Mr. Wilde's disappointment with the Atlantic" went the country over. His personal appearance at this time was that of a tall, strongly built, somewhat heavy figure, with a smooth, oval face, and flowing locks. His dress, always distinctive and marked, differed from the usual commonplace type by reason of a soft felt hat, a voluminous cloak or cape, a floating crimson necktie and a velvet jacket. He was taken to a hotel for breakfast, and thence to private apartments, and his address kept secret. In the six days before his address he received many flattering marks of attention from those who had met him abroad, and he attended one or two dinners and two receptions, one given by Mrs. Croly (Jennie June), and the other at the house of Mr. A. A. Hayes, then one of the "gilded youth" of New York society.

On the night of the lecture, January 9, just before his entrance, Mr. Wilde was perfectly cool and collected—not nervous, as many of the most prominent speakers often are. Probably the most trying ordeal of the whole evening was the first few minutes of his entrance on the stage at Chickering Hall, when a wait to seat late comers made him the focus of the eyes of the house. His costume was the court suit of the English private gentleman, a fine closely-fitting velvet coat with wide flowing skirts, a close waistcoat with lace at bosom and sleeves, knee breeches, silk stockings, and buckled shoes.

My announcement of the title of Mr. Wilde's address was the only introduction made. What Mr. Wilde said, and how he said it, has been chronicled by many different pens and repeated with many varying comments. From the stage, facing the audience, it was curious and interesting to note the changing and varying expressions of the people—first, of open, frank curiosity, then whispered comments and veiled sarcasms could be heard, and in some of the back upper seats, open ridicule. But at the end of the first five minutes, devoted to defining his purpose, the charm of Mr. Wilde's voice, his novel and picturesque diction, and the simplicity and clearness of his address, caught the people off their guard, and a kind of gasp of astonishment and incredulity swept over the house. As he went on, the calm, persuasive, convincing manner of the man had its effect, and when he came to the place where he appealed from Gilbert to Wilde, from æstheticism as caricatured on the stage by Bunthorne, to himself, and his meaning of what he believed to be the true æsthetic, artistic spirit, his audience was captured, and applauded to the echo. Even his reference to the flowers of the æsthetic movement, the sunflower and lily, was taken in the spirit of the speaker, not the actor that travestied him.

This trial before a critical, supercilious, almost hostile audience, defined his place as a public speaker, and there was never afterwards a question as to the man's position and power over his hearers, if he could once get them to listen quietly. In a somewhat extended experience in business relations with public speakers of the first rank of America and England, there is no instance in the writer's judgment of so severe a trial or a more complete and convincing success than was made by Mr. Wilde at his first appearance before an American audience.

After a short interval occupied by a round of receptions, dinners, and attentions that were forced upon him, Mr. Wilde began the itinerary of lectures that had been arranged for him.

It so happened that at Baltimore and Washington the lectures of Mr. Forbes, arranged for long in advance, came just before the visit of Mr. Wilde. In speaking at Baltimore, Mr. Forbes made some passing allusion to the coming of Mr. Wilde and his "mission," not intended as anything more than a casual remark on what was then a popular topic of the day. This was reported by some officious and malicious person to Mr. Wilde, and he sent a letter to Mr. Forbes, which created a "state of things." Mr. Forbes demanded an apology, threatening to attack Wilde in the public prints and in person. Wilde was stubborn, angry, and satirical, and refused to recede. Mr. Carte was in Florida; communication by wire was not easy. It took some active work, no little patience, and a deal of diplomatic persuasion, and a cable from Mr.

George Lewis, of London, to calm the excited spirits and restore peace.   Lewis cabled finally, January 28:

"Like a good fellow, don't attack Wilde.   I ask this personal favour to me."

It was at Washington that Mr. Wilde first came across the personal caricatures that afterwards frequently announced his advent in other places.   The *Post* printed two pictures—of a man that bore some resemblance to the lecturer, and an ape—and the caption, "From this to this."   This was protested against by the writer, and was strongly commented upon as a boorish exhibition of bad taste by other papers.

The Boston lecture, the fourth in the series, was perhaps the most pronounced personal victory Mr. Wilde ever achieved. The arrangements were made with the proprietor of the Boston Music Hall, the largest auditorium in the city, and all the preliminary work of announcement was done by him. Just an hour before the lecture an intimation was made that many Harvard students would attend in costume and give Mr. Wilde a reception of their own.

A suggestion was made to Mr. Wilde that the æsthetic costume be omitted that night, and he was advised as to an intended attempt of the students to embarrass him. After the hall was filled, and fifty students in many ludicrous imitations of æsthetic costumes occupied the front seats, they were warned that any demonstration that would interfere with the progress of the lecture or tend to cause a panic in the audience would be promptly suppressed.

The stage was very wide, a long walk from the back to the reading desk in front. Mr. Wilde, alone, slowly and quietly walked down the stage, placed his manuscript on the desk, smilingly faced the rows of surprised students, and, addressing them directly, assured them of his very great satisfaction and pleasure in seeing so many fellow collegians present to honor him, complimented them with perfect seriousness on their picturesque attire and attitudes, and went on to tell them something of his own college experience in his Oxford days when making roads with Ruskin. He then turned quietly to his desk and began with the lecture, to the accompanying applause of the audience. There were no interruptions from the front rows of seats, but hearty applause arose when

Mr. Wilde offered a Greek statue of an athlete for the university gymnasium. Mr. Wilde's tact and dignified and courteous bearing disarmed the opposition, and some sarcastic thrusts made in the course of the lecture sufficiently punished the students for their early discourtesy.

Mr. Wilde returned to Boston some months later and gave an address in the Boston Theatre to an afternoon audience, largely of ladies, upon "Dress and Art in Home Decorations," which was enthusiastically received. It was at this time he visited Cambridge, and was paid many attentions from the very men who had tried to ridicule him on his first appearance.

The lecture tour of Mr. Wilde was now fairly begun, and after appearing in Philadelphia he proceeded west to Albany, Rochester, Buffalo, and Chicago, where two addresses were made. From Chicago he visited St. Paul and several smaller places en route to Omaha, Denver, and the Pacific coast. Here he gave four lectures, as by this time he had prepared additional ones on "Art Decoration" and on the "Art of Dress." After San Francisco he returned East, stopping at several cities and repeating in others the new addresses. This tour, including nearly all of the larger American towns, was arranged by the writer from New York.

Throughout this lecture tour Mr. Wilde was accompanied by Mr. J. H. Vail, who was his travelling manager. Many places visited were, as yet, but little acquainted with the ideas and purposes of the æsthetic movement, and here the lectures were received with little enthusiasm. The newspapers were prompt to seize upon the prominent points of the lecture, but usually gave the greatest space to personal descriptions of the man, his dress and demeanor, and occasionally indulged in humor at his expense.

It was during this western trip that Mr. Wilde accumulated a fund of stories, racy of the soil, that served as a background, often as material, for adventures that afterwards amused his audiences in the bohemian circles of the English and French capitals.

Many of the newspapers recognized the value of the ideas advanced by Mr. Wilde, though often proclaiming them to be utterly above the common comprehension. But there can be no doubt of the fact that the lectures were a strong force for improvement in house and home artistic decoration.

Towards the last Mr. Wilde was outspoken in

satirizing the crude and inartistic combinations of color and objects in architecture, dress, and furnishing, and suggested ideas that unquestionably helped to improve and develop a more artistic and cultured home atmosphere. His lectures were always of the greatest interest to women. Men, unless cultured and students, rarely took much notice of the new gospel of art. His most attentive listeners were women, and to them his views came often as a new revelation.

On returning from the West, Mr. Wilde visited Canada, speaking at Montreal, Quebec, Ottawa, Kingston, Toronto, and some smaller towns. This was to him the most enjoyable part of his tour. Here was a new field, more congenial in many ways than the American towns, and with audiences more in sympathy with the man and his subjects. His powers were at their best, the constant work of the preceding months had given him confidence and skill in delivery, and shown him the weak places to be avoided in public addresses. His subject was "The House Beautiful," something more tangible and understandable than the spirituelle ideas of æsthetic beauty he had heretofore expounded. There was also an afternoon lecture on "Dress and Manners," especially interesting to the ladies.

The audiences were large and enthusiastic, the papers reported him accurately and fully.   There
were numberless entertainments, receptions, and
interviews without end.   The appended appreciative letter from one of the leading literary men
of Toronto shows exactly the impression he made:

Evening News, Toronto, Thursday, May 25, '82.

OSCAR WILDE.

SIR: Coming up from the Capital yesterday,
when seated at breakfast, in a far from æsthetic
mood, who should be seated next to me but the
renowned apostle of the beautiful, Mr. Oscar
Wilde.   Trusting to the freemasonry of sympathetic ideas, I introduced myself as the friend of
the late M———, one of the most gifted art critics
of this generation, and the joint author with him
of certain sketches of the Old Masters.   We were
at once *en rapport,* and I found that I had by this
allusion, as the prophet in the wilderness by his
rod made the waters to gush out, touched a copious
spring of highly cultured intelligence, philosophical reflection, and acute criticism, both humorous
and eloquent.   Mr. Wilde is a brilliant conversa-

tionalist, a happy one in all senses, for he can
listen as well as he can talk, and he can talk so
that listening to his tongue, even to the garrulous,
becomes more pleasant than to listen to their own.
Well, although I am not garrulous, I can prevent
talk dropping into silence, and I listened yesterday
morning to the only conversation worthy the name
which I have had the privilege to share in since
leaving England many years ago, for, unhappily,
here we cannot find anything to chat over save the
virtues of our party and the wickedness of the
opposite one, which is not a sufficiently varied
theme to monopolise *all* one's lingual social capacity or mental sympathies. To my mind, one of the
greatest disadvantages of life in Canada is the
blank, the utter blank, of the charm of intellectual
gossip. My talk with Mr. Wilde took me out of
the dust and smoke and clatter of a noisy, monotonous street into the heart of the country, rich in
woodland beauty, redolent of floral sweetness, and
soothing to the tired brain as a mother's lullaby
to her child. We talked of art, of its present aspects here and at home; of art culture, of art
schools, and their work and failures and needs.
I told Mr. Wilde that years ago I had ventured
to lay down as the glaring defect of all Canadian

pictures that they showed an entire want of the power of drawing with exactitude any living forms, trees, or animals. This he earnestly and almost passionately approved. "Art," said he, "is not looked upon as an exact science, as it should be; there can be no art without truth of form, and no beauty can exist where is falsehood in drawing or colour." He then went on very suggestively, and with a delicacy of allusion to my own expressions which indicated the refinement of high breeding (for Mr. Wilde is a gentleman to the core), to insist that no true appreciation of form, or capacity to express it in any aspect, figure, drawing, or architecture, can exist unless there is in the draughtsman a keen, clear, pure conception and vivid sense of the charm and value of colour. A position which, though it will be "caviare to the general," and not acceptable to many artists and architects, is, I believe, demonstrable. He heartily sympathised with and pushed to a humorous conclusion my ridicule of the ordinary methods of teaching in so-called Art Schools, their uselessness, their chilling and repressing effect upon the young. We then struck off at a tangent into a discussion as to the relative merits of Thackeray and Dickens, in which Mr. Wilde displayed, for so young a man, a remarkable familiarity with the whole field of fictional literature. He condemned freely the historical novels of Scott, as in the conversations of the characters stilted and unnatural; he placed Bulwer's historical romances on a lower level still, and, in doing so, used a phrase which is worth quoting. "Romance," said he, "what is it but humanity in its nobler, finer phases?" To be truly romantic, therefore, is not to be unnatural, for that is to be false to nature, but it is to take human life into a higher expression and mood. Back again to art, we discussed the prevailing bad work done by artisans, the craze for cheap work and its results in degrading work and workers. His vehement condemnation of the preference given by young men for such occupations as clerks in stores, or any similar work, over handicrafts, was to me most refreshing, as sweet, indeed, to hear as the red-hot gospel of a revivalist's thunder is to the religious fanatic.

Here he struck upon a vein of reflection, that the so-called "working classes," that is, handicraftsmen, will have to work before their social emancipation day dawns, their freedom from a ban which nowadays settles upon them, chiefly as the result of their own want of respect for their occupations. Mr. Wilde, with much fire and with graphic illustrations, touched upon the artistic aspect, and claims to art treatment of the ordinary artisan's work. "To be done well," said he, "work must be done truly; and, done with truth, it becomes artistic. This element of faithfulness is the only power able to raise labour into honour." The thought is, of course, not original, but how few, how very few, see clearly wherein really consists the difference between work worthy of being respected, and which will bring respect to the worker, and work which is not respected, work of which the doer is made to feel that the very doing of it is in a sense a degradation. In a word, I found Mr. Oscar Wilde a man of high useful capacity, wide reading and observation, clear-headed, practical in his views as to the relation of worthy ends to fitting means to attain them, with deep, earnest sympathies with the socially depressed, and an almost passionate longing for the spread of refined tastes and habits among the humbler classes; an enthusiast, doubtless, but enthusiasm has done every good work yet done in this world, and one who, in spite of some eccentricities—for all enthusiasts have been eccentric—is doing, and will yet do, I believe and hope, a thoroughly good work in that sphere to which he deems himself called, the sphere of art reformer and teacher.

JOHN HAGUE.

Mr. Wilde returned to New York at the end of May to arrange, if possible, for the production of his play, "Vera, the Nihilist." The play was privately printed under my copyright, and sent to several of the leading actors and managers for consideration, but no definite arrangements could then be made for it.

The first tour of Mr. Wilde was brought to an end in May, 1882. There were then no regular lectures in summer, except at the Chautauqua associations, and these courses were already filled. It was suggested that some knowledge of the American summer life at the watering places would be of interest to Mr. Wilde, as continuing his study of the American people under different aspects and surroundings.

A summer tour was mapped out, in which the writer accompanied Mr. Wilde to Newport, Saratoga, Richfield Springs, Sharon Springs, The Catskills, Long Branch, Atlantic City, Cape May, and several smaller places. This was a unique experience, bringing Mr. Wilde into closer touch with the popular life of the American summer season. There was plenty of time for the observation of scenery, the journeys were not hurried, there was no urgency, and the leisurely progress from one point to another, after the rapid and fatiguing hurry of the previous railway journeys, was delightfully resting.

In these summer addresses Mr. Wilde was at his best. He had no longer to depend upon his manuscript, but varied his talks to suit the occasion, and often to suit the audience. Some of these addresses were far more interesting than the more formal affairs of the platform. The afternoon meetings, when his audiences were ladies, in charming toilettes, were a source of inspiration to the speaker, and responded to by the enthusiastic yet subdued applause of his hearers. They sparkled with wit, epigram and metaphor; the illustrations were drawn from his own observations and later experiences; the higher intelligence of his audiences, appreciative of his best efforts, incited him to flights of fancy and oratory not reached before. Unfortunately, none were ever adequately reported or preserved.

With the coming of the fall months, to complete the tour of the States and Provinces, a short lecture tour was arranged in October, 1882. Mr. Wilde, with Mr. Husted as his manager, left for New England, and after speaking at Portland and Bangor, Maine, arrived at St. Johns, N. B., October 4, speaking there October 6.

The Provincial papers were uniformly courteous and the lectures were treated with great respect and reported at length. There were many attentions shown Mr. Wilde by the hospitable people, and all seemed to be anxious to do him honor.

There have been several misstatements as to management and returns for the lectures of Mr. Wilde. At no time was Major Pond connected with his lectures. The facts are, that these lectures of Mr. Wilde during the eight months which he devoted to them in America, were very remunerative, both to himself and his management. There is no warrant for the report that the tours were abandoned before completion. Every engagement was carried out. If postponed by reason of stress of weather or illness, they were afterwards filled. The sums paid to Mr. Wilde passed through the writer's hands, and very considerable amounts were remitted to England during his stay here. At the end a substantial and ample com-

pensation was paid him. Even his summer lectures, something that had very rarely before been
undertaken here, netted him a considerable return
for two months of a pleasure trip, for it was really
nothing more than a summer outing. The figures
are at hand to show that his honorarium for the
year spent in America was what was then a large
sum for any foreign lecturer, and even now would
be considered quite satisfactory to any speaker of
the first rank. His travelling expenses were always
large, for nothing was spared to make the journeys
comfortable and to supply every need and lux-
ury. The arrangements made by Mr. Carte were
liberal, and were lived up to, and certainly, to the
positive knowledge of the writer, who had control
of the entire tours from beginning to end, there
was no cause for complaint or heart-burning on
either side.

Much might be said of the personal habits, demeanor, and behavior of Mr. Wilde during the
period of this American visit. Meeting, as he did,
with a misconception of the true message which
he brought and taught—and with a critical, biased,
often hostile and condemnatory press against him
—subject to misapprehension by a public which
could not always clearly comprehend or assimilate

what he said, it was a trial that would have taxed
the powers of an older, more experienced and ma-
ture man to the uttermost limit of his strength.
It is not to the purpose to inquire just how far
he at first allowed himself to fill the place popularly given him, as a mere poseur, an affected in-
carnation of a passing fad; the facts remain the
same—that the direct result of the lectures, writings, interviews, and talks of this young man had
a strong and distinct effect upon the æsthetic, artistic and ethical sense of the people of this country, an effect which perhaps few are willing to
acknowledge, but which has, nevertheless, left its
imprint upon the national life and is felt for a
better and higher national culture.

The effect of this year of hard work upon
Mr. Wilde was distinctly and strongly for his
good. He had, at the end, broadened and developed, grown stronger, more self-reliant, had seen
the unwisdom of the shallow affectations that at
first controlled his actions, and come at the last
to realize there was something in life better worth
while than to wear the mask of a poseur and mas-
querader.

The titles of the lectures and addresses delivered by Mr. Wilde when in this country have often

been misquoted. The first formal lecture delivered in New York City was entitled "The English Renaissance." This was frequently reported in the papers at length, and was reprinted, evidently from the newspaper reports, in the "Sea Side Library," in January, 1882. The lecture was typewritten, bound in a morocco case, and was never suffered to pass out of the possession of Mr. Wilde or his manager. The original notes were destroyed when the lecture was typewritten.

In February, at Chicago, Mr. Wilde prepared a second address, which he delivered from notes. Afterwards the lecture was carefully written out and was entitled "The Decorative Arts." This lecture proved to be the most popular, and was oftenest in demand. It was delivered generally on second nights in a course or at matinees. During the month of March Mr. Wilde wrote me: "Kindly see that I am not advertised to lecture on 'The English Renaissance.' I have not delivered that lecture since February 11, and yet I am always advertised for it. It is very annoying, and besides, 'The English Renaissance' is printed in the 'Sea Side,' so people think they know it, and stay away. The lecture is on 'The Decorative Arts.' "

The words "in America" were never added by

Mr. Wilde to this lecture, though the title is often quoted as "The Decorative Arts in America," or "Decorative Art in America."

Later in the tour there was need for still another lecture for the afternoons, and so on April 1, at San Francisco, the title announced for a Saturday matinee was "The House Beautiful and Art Decoration."

From Chicago Mr. Wilde wrote: "I hope you will arrange some more matinees; to lecture in the day does not tire me. I would sooner lecture five or six times a week, and travel, say, three or four hours a day, than lecture three times and travel ten hours. I do not think I should ever lecture less than four times, and these matinees are a great hit. Let me know what we are to do after Cincinnati—is it Canada? I am ready to lecture till last week in April—April 15, say."

But it was not always possible to arrange for matinees, and the long journeys had to be made. But there were intervals of rest arranged to be passed in the larger cities, when possible. The lay-offs appeared to be popular with the newspaper fraternity, for an interview with Oscar Wilde was always good copy.

On his return from the West Mr. Wilde repeated

in New York, at Wallack's Theatre, on May 11,
the lecture then announced as "Art Decoration."
The New York *Tribune* gave a full report of the
lecture and introduced the report as follows:

ART DECORATION.

MR. WILDE'S SECOND LECTURE IN NEW YORK.

A LARGE AUDIENCE IN WALLACK'S THEATRE—NO
    MANUSCRIPT USED BY THE LECTURER—HIS
    DRESS AND MANNER.

Wallack's Theatre was well filled yesterday afternoon, when Oscar Wilde delivered his lecture on
"Art Decoration." Several of the boxes were occupied by parties of ladies, and a few heads appeared
over the edge of the second balcony. A tall ebony
pedestal stood in the centre of the stage, and on
it was a glass of water. The scene set represented
a library finished in modern Gothic style. Bric-à-
brac in large quantities from art stores, and numerous paper vases from the property-room of
the theatre were placed around indiscriminately.
Mr. Wilde walked on the stage shortly before three
o'clock, and was applauded with the decorum that

was characteristic of the audience and its manner from first to last. The lecturer wore a new suit, consisting of dark velvet coat and knee breeches, with a profusion of lace around the neck, down the front, and at the cuffs. He had on dark stockings and patent-leather pumps.

Mr. Wilde spoke for an hour and twenty minutes without notes. At first he assumed an attitude which has been made familiar by his full-length photographs, and maintained it, with occasional lapses into gracefulness, until he had finished. He spoke in a monotonous tone of voice, like a schoolboy reciting a lesson, and suffered from occasional failures of memory. In such cases he hurried on without a halt to a new series of observations. He repeated himself to some extent. In the arrangement of his discourse there was little of the "rational designs" whose necessity he sought so earnestly to impress on his hearers. He ended abruptly, and the audience did not know that he had finished until he bowed and was leaving the stage. Then a lady threw a lily from her box. The audience applauded, and as the lecturer returned he was greeted with a bunch of Jacque-minot roses. He picked them up, again bowed his acknowledgments, and retired. The receipts were estimated to be $900, which is less by $300 than at his first lecture in New York. P. T. Barnum was present and occupied a front seat.

THE LECTURE.

In my first lecture I gave you something of the history of Art in England. I sought to trace the influence of the French Revolution upon its development. I said something of the song of Keats and the school of the pre-Raphaelites. But I do not want to shelter the movement which I have called "The English Renaissance" under any palladium, however noble, or any name, however revered. The roots of it have indeed to be sought for in things that have long passed away, and not, as some suppose, in the fancy of a few young men, although I am not altogether sure that there is anything much better than the fancy of a few young men. When I appeared before you on a previous occasion I had seen nothing of American art save the Doric columns and Corinthian chimney-pots visible on your Broadway and Fifth Avenue. Since then I have been through your country to some fifty or sixty cities, I think. I find that what your people need is not so much high imaginative art, but that which hallows the vessels of every-day use. I suppose that the poet will sing, and the artist will paint, regardless whether the world praises or blames. He has his own world and is independent of his fellow-men. But the handicraftsman is dependent on your pleasure and opinion. He needs your encouragement, and he must have beautiful surroundings. Your people love art, but you do not sufficiently honor the handicraftsman. Of course, those millionaires who can pillage Europe for their pleasure need have no care to encourage such; but I speak for those whose desire for beautiful things is larger than their means. I find that one great trouble all over is that your workmen are not given to noble designs. You cannot be indifferent to this, because art is not something which you can take or leave. It is a necessity of human life.

And what is the meaning of this beautiful decoration which we call art? In the first place, it means value to the workman, and it means the pleasure which he must necessarily take in making a beautiful thing. The mark of all good art is not that the thing done is done exactly or finely, for machinery may do as much; but that it is worked out with the head and the workman's heart. I cannot impress the point too frequently that beautiful and rational designs are necessary in all work. I did not imagine until I went into some of your simpler cities that there was so much bad work done. I found where I went bad wall-papers, horribly designed and colored carpets, and that old offender, the horse-hair sofa, whose stolid look of indifference is always so depressing. I found meaningless chandeliers and machine-made furniture, generally of rosewood, which creaked dismally under the weight of the ubiquitous interviewer. I came across the small iron stove which they always persist in decorating with machine-made ornaments, and which is as great a bore as a wet day, or any other particularly dreadful institution. When unusual extravagance was indulged in it was garnished with two funeral urns.

BRING ARTIST AND WORKMAN TOGETHER.

It must always be remembered that what is well and carefully made by an honest workman after a rational design increases in beauty and value as the years go on. The old furniture brought over by the Pilgrims 200 years ago, which I saw in New England, is just as good and as beautiful to-day as it was when it first came here. Now what you must do is to bring artists and handicraftsmen together. Handicraftsmen cannot live, certainly cannot thrive, without such companionship. Separate these two, and you rob art of all spiritual motive. Having done this, you must place your workman in the midst of beautiful surroundings. The artist is not dependent on the visible and the tangible. He has his visions and his dreams to feed on. But the workman must see lovely forms and beautiful forms as he goes to his work in the morning and returns at eventide. And, in connection with this, I want to assure you that noble and beautiful designs are never the result of idle fancy or purposeless day-dreaming. They only come as the accumulation of habits of long and delightful observation. And yet such things may not be taught. Right ideas concerning them can certainly only be obtained by those who have been accustomed to rooms that are beautiful and colors that are satisfying.

Perhaps one of the most difficult things for us to do is to choose a notable and joyous dress for men. There would be more joy in life if we should accustom ourselves to use all the beautiful colors we can in fashioning our own clothes. The dress

of the future, I think, will use drapery to a great
extent, and will abound with joyous color.   At
present we have lost all nobility of dress, and in
doing so have almost annihilated the modern sculptor.   And in looking around at the figures which
adorn our parks one could almost wish that we had
completely killed the noble art.   To see the frock
coat of the drawing-room done into bronze, or the
double waistcoat perpetuated in marble, adds a
new horror to death.   But indeed, in looking
through the history of costume, seeking an answer
to the questions we have propounded, there is little that is either beautiful or appropriate.   One
of the earliest forms is the Greek drapery, which
is so exquisite for young girls.   And then, I think
we may be pardoned a little enthusiasm over the
dress of the time of Charles I, so beautiful, indeed,
that in spite of its invention being with the cava-
liers, it was copied by the Puritans.   And the dress
for the children at that time must not be passed
over.   It was a very golden age of the little ones.
I do not think that they have ever looked so lovely
as they do in the pictures of that time.   The dress
of the last century in England is also peculiarly
gracious and graceful.   There is nothing bizarre
or strange about it, but it is full of harmony and

beauty. In these days, when we have suffered so dreadfully from the incursions of the modern milliner, we hear ladies boast that they do not wear a dress more than once. In the old days, when the dresses were decorated with beautiful designs and worked with exquisite embroidery, ladies rather took a pride in bringing out the garment and wearing it many times, and handing it down to their daughters, a process which I think would be quite appreciated by modern husbands when called upon to settle their wives' bills.

HOW MEN SHOULD DRESS.

And how shall men dress? Men say they don't particularly care how they dress, and that it is little matter. I am bound to reply that I do not believe them, and do not think that you do. In all my journeys through the country, the only well dressed men that I saw—and in saying this I earnestly deprecate the polished indignation of your Fifth Avenue dandies—were the Western miners. Their wide-brimmed hats, which shaded their faces from the sun and protected them from the rain, and the cloak, which is by far the most beautiful piece of drapery ever invented, may well

be dwelt on with admiration. Their high boots,
too, were sensible and practical. They only wore
what was comfortable, and, therefore, beautiful.
As I looked at them I could not help thinking with
regret of the time when these picturesque miners
should have made their fortunes and would go East
to assume again all the abominations of modern
fashionable attire. Indeed, so concerned was I that
I made some of them promise that when they
again appeared in the more crowded scenes of
Eastern civilization they would still continue to
wear their lovely costume. But I don't believe
they will.

Now, what America wants to-day is a school
of rational design. Bad art is a great deal worse
than no art at all. You must show your workmen
specimens of good work, so that they may come
to know what is simple and true and beautiful. To
that end I would have you have a museum attached
to these schools—not one of those dreadful modern
institutions where there are a stuffed and very
dusty giraffe and a case or two of fossils, but a
place where there are gathered examples of art decoration from various periods and countries. Such
a place is the South Kensington Museum in London, whereon we build greater hopes for the future

than on any other one thing. There I go every Saturday night, when the Museum is open later than usual, to see the handicraftsman, the woodworker, the glassblower, and the worker in metals. And it is here that the man of refinement and culture comes face to face with the workman who ministers to his joy. He comes to know more of the nobility of the workman, and the workman, feeling the appreciation, comes to know more of the nobility of his work.

You have too many white walls. More color is wanted. You should have such men as Whistler among you, to teach you the beauty and joy of color. Take Mr. Whistler's symphony in white, which you no doubt have imagined to be something quite bizarre. It is nothing of the sort. Think of a cool, gray sky, flecked here and there with white clouds, a gray ocean and three wonderfully beautiful figures robed in white leaning over the water and dropping white flowers from their fingers. Here are no extensive intellectual scheme to trouble you, and no metaphysics, of which we have had quite enough in art. But if the simple and unaided color strikes the right keynote, the whole conception is made clear. I regard Mr. Whistler's famous peacock room as the finest thing

in color and art decoration which the world has
known since Correggio painted that wonderful
room in Italy where the little children are dancing
on the walls. Mr. Whistler finished another room
just before I came away—a breakfast room in blue
and yellow. The ceiling was light blue, the cabinet
furniture was of yellow wood, the curtains at the
windows were white and worked in yellow, and
when the table was set for breakfast with dainty
blue china, nothing can be conceived at once so
simple and joyous.

The fault which I have observed in most of your
room is that there is apparent no definite scheme
of color. Everything is not attuned to a keynote
as it should be. The apartments are crowded with
pretty things which have no relation with each
other. Again, your artists must decorate what is
more simply useful. In your art schools I found
no attempt to decorate such things as the vessels
for water. I know of nothing uglier than the ordinary jug or pitcher. A museum could be filled
with the different kinds of water vessels which
are used in hot countries. Yet we continue to
submit to the depressing jug with the handle all
on one side. I do not see the wisdom of decorating dinner plates with sunsets, and soup plates

with moonlight scenes. I do not think it adds anything to the pleasure of a canvasback duck to take it out of such glories. Besides, we do not want a soup plate whose bottom seems to vanish in the distance. One neither feels safe nor comfortable under such conditions. In fact, I did not find in the art schools of the country that the difference was explained between decorative and imaginative art.

THE CONDITIONS OF ART.

The conditions of art should be simple. A great deal more depends upon the heart than the head. Appreciation of art is not secured by any elaborate scheme of learning. Art requires a good healthy atmosphere. The motives for art are still around about us as they were around about the ancients. And the subjects are also easily found by the earnest sculptor and painter. Nothing is more picturesque and graceful than a man at work. Only idle people are ungraceful. The artist who goes to the children's playground, watches them at their sport, sees the boy stoop to tie his shoe, will find the same themes that engaged the attention of the ancient Greeks. And such observation and the

illustrations which follow will do much to correct
that foolish impression that mental and physical
beauty are always divorced.

To you more than perhaps to any other country
has nature been generous in furnishing mate-
rials for art workers to work in.   You have marble
quarries, where the stone is more beautiful in color
than the Greeks ever had for their beautiful work,
and yet day after day I am confronted with the
great building of some stupid man who has used
the beautiful material as if it were not precious
almost beyond speech.   Marble should not be used
save by noble workmen.   There is nothing which
gave me a greater sense of barrenness in travelling
through the country than the entire absence of
wood carving on your houses.   Wood carving is
the simplest of the decorative arts.   In Switzer-
land the little barefooted boy beautifies the porch
of his father's house with examples of skill in this
direction.   Why should not American boys do a
great deal more and better than Swiss boys?

There is nothing to my mind more coarse in
conception and more vulgar in execution than
modern jewelry.   This is something that can be
easily corrected.   Something better should be made
out of the beautiful gold which is stored up in

your mountain hollows and strewn along your river beds. When I was at Leadville, and reflected that all the shining silver I saw coming from the mines would be made into ugly dollars, it made me sad. It should be made into something more permanent. The golden gates at Florence are as beautiful to-day as when Michael Angelo saw them.

We should see more of the workman than we do. We should not be content to have the salesman stand between us, who knows nothing of what he is selling save that he is charging a great deal too much for it. And watching workmen will teach that most important lesson, the nobility of all rational workmanship.

THE PLACE OF ART IN EDUCATION

I said in my last lecture that art would create a new brotherhood among men by furnishing a universal language. I said that under its beneficent influences war might pass away. Thinking this, what place can I ascribe to art in our education? If children grow up among all fair and lovely things, they will grow to love beauty and detest ugliness before they know the reason why. If you go into a house where everything is coarse you find things chipped and broken and unsightly. Nobody exercises any care. If everything is dainty and delicate, gentleness and refinement of manner are unconsciously acquired. When I was in San Francisco I used to visit the Chinese quarters frequently. There I used to watch a great hulking Chinese workman at his task of digging, and used to see him every day drink his tea from a little cup as delicate in texture as the petal of a flower. Whereas in all the grand hotels of the land, where thousands of dollars have been lavished on great gilt mirrors and gaudy columns, I have been given my coffee or my chocolate in cups an inch and a quarter thick. I think I have deserved something nicer. [Laughter.]

The art systems of the past have been devised by philosophers who looked upon human beings as abstractions. They have tried to educate boys' minds before they had any. How much better it would be in these early years to teach children to use their hands in the rational service of mankind! I would have a workshop attached to every school, and one hour a day given up to the teaching of simple decorative arts. It would be a golden hour to the children. And you would soon raise up a race of handicraftsmen who would transform the face of your country. I have seen only one such school in the United States, and this was in Philadelphia, and was founded by my friend Mr. Leland. I stopped there yesterday, and have brought some of their work here this afternoon to show you. [Mr. Wilde here turned from the stand to an adjoining table and held up the different articles he spoke of.] Here are two discs of beaten brass; the designs on them are beautiful, the workmanship is simple, and the entire result is satisfactory. The work was done by a little boy twelve years old. This is a wooden bowl decorated by a little girl of thirteen. The design is lovely, and the coloring delicate and pretty. [The bowl was painted black and yellow, and looked like a sunflower with the colors run into each other.] Here you see a piece of beautiful wood carving, accomplished by a little boy of nine. [This was a small, rectangular piece of wood, and the carving was not visible to the audience.] In such work as this children learn sincerity in art. They learn to abhor the liar in art—the man who paints wood to look like iron, or iron to look like stone. It is a practical school of morals. [Applause.] No better way is there to learn to love nature than to understand art. It dignifies every flower of the field.

And a boy who sees the thing of beauty which a bird on the wing becomes when transferred to wood or canvas will probably not throw the customary stone. What we want is something spiritual added to life. Nothing is so ignoble that art cannot sanctify it.

On the Canadian tour which followed the second visit to New York Mr. Wilde gave as the title of his lecture "The Decorative Arts," and at matinees he gave "The House Beautiful and Home Decoration." The tour of New England and Canada occupied the fall of 1882 and closed the series of lectures in this country.

During the first visit to America I copyrighted under my name Mr. Wilde's play, "Vera, the Nihilist," and fifty copies were printed for private use. I suggested this course to Mr. Wilde, and received from him the following letter, written at the time Mr. Wilde was lecturing in Boston, and bearing the date, January 31, 1882:

"Thank you for sending the play to Washington. I think to copyright under your name would be a very good plan. I wish you would send one to the manager you spoke of here, Mr. Field, also one to

Rose Coghlan, at Wallack's, and one to Wallack himself; also one to Mr. Henderson. I think he might try it. I wish you would tell Heyman Haynes that I accept his offer for next October, 1883. That will be exactly good and convenient."

The copies of "Vera," twelve in all, were distributed by me as directed by Mr. Wilde. The remainder were delivered to Mr. Wilde by me personally on his return to New York.

The newspaper comments and criticisms of Mr. Wilde and his lectures during his American tour are a curious commentary upon the man and his mission. Nearly always in advance of Mr. Wilde's coming the preliminary notices were sarcastic and sneering, or even good-natured raillery at the man and his message. Upon Mr. Wilde's arrival at the town in which he was to lecture the reporters met him, and often there appeared admirable pen portraits of the lecturer. After the lecture a summary of the chief points was generally given in a more or less accurate manner, and generally at the end of the summary there was a confession that there was more truth and less poetry and romance in the lecture than had been expected.

The following extracts from two newspapers are quoted as indicative of the attitude of many at the beginning of Mr. Wilde's lecture tour, as set forth in the Washington *Post* of January 24, 1882, and the saner judgment which may truthfully be said to represent the prevailing tone of the press toward the end of Mr. Wilde's tour, as set forth by the Montreal *Daily Witness* of May 15, 1882:

Washington Post, January 24, 1882.

ÆSTHETIC SYLLABUB.

OSCAR WILDE'S LECTURE AT LINCOLN HALL LAST NIGHT.

HOW THE MAN LOOKED AND TALKED—A COMMONPLACE PERFORMANCE AND AN UNAPPRECIATIVE AUDIENCE—ART AND POETRY.

The appearance of Oscar Wilde upon the stage at Lincoln Hall, last night, caused a polite æsthetic rustle in the audience, which did not develop, however, into a vulgar titter. This was due possibly to the fact that Oscar was not arrayed in his gorgeous pea-green coat and brown velvet knee-breeches, which usually make him conspicuous when he appears in public. His knee-breeches, of course, were not lacking, but they were dark in hue, and the rest of his costume was comparatively quiet—dark, sombre, Rembrandtic, mediæval, so to speak. The upper half of his person resembled an English curate—his lower extremities an Italian brigand. He wore black silk stockings and black knee-breeches, which gave his legs a general and remote resemblance to two sticks of licorice. The lecture was delivered throughout in sing-songy, languidly drawling tones, the voice ascending and descending at regular intervals, and the sentences ending with a rising inflection. At first the audience, despite the fact that the speaker could hardly be heard, seemed inclined to be attentive, but patience soon ceased to be a virtue. Then opera-glasses were directed to all parts of the hall except the stage, ladies yawned, the gentlemen looked bored, and at last so many arose and left that at times the sound of the speaker's voice was drowned. In his favorite position, the lecturer stood with one hand resting on the desk before him and the other crooked against his side, his body meanwhile leaning at an angle of thirty degrees to the perpendicular. Only his left hand was gloved, and his right caressed the other glove with a soft, poetic fervor.

Mr. Wilde's features, of which the picture in the *Sunday Post* was a faithful copy, were occasionally relaxed by a sickly, almost imbecile smile. This was when he said something that he thought was rather pretty, or when, by adroitly appealing to national pride, he secured a little applause. His manner is mild and deliberative, and he announces the most startling facts and astounding theories with an innocent nonchalance that is perfectly delicious. He talked about revolutions and faïence in the same breath, and skipped from the harmonies of the soul to Japanese wickerwork with the utmost agility. The whole character of the lecture is kaleidoscopic, if not slightly mixed. Keats and Goethe, carved doorways and painted chests are delightfully combined with Achilles and the Duke of Wellington. There is a kind of boyish simplicity about him that absolutely disarms serious criticism, as when he says that "the first duty of a critic is to keep silent upon all occasions and on all subjects"—a remark that comes much nearer a bull than a witticism. As a lecture his performance is severely commonplace. It has a good deal of Ruskin and Goethe, flavored with Burne-Jones and Swinburne, and largely diluted with Oscar Wilde, and is perfectly harmless.

"I have not come to America with sinister motives," Mr. Wilde condescended to say, "but rather to try to tell you exactly what we are doing in England for art, that you may at least understand it, whether you praise it or not." The audience would have been glad if, in the first place, it could have understood what the lecturer was endeavoring to drive at. He commenced with telling the story of the pre-Raphaelites, who, he said, were a group of young men, possessing youth, power and enthusiasm—three things which the English public could not tolerate. His remark that "Satire—always as impudent as it is insolent—paid them the usual homage which mediocrity pays to genius," was thought to be a hit back at those who ridicule the æsthetic craze. The first applause which the lecturer received was elicited by a reference to a piece of advice which Walt Whitman had given him about writing poetry. And the second was when he alluded to Poe. He was saying that the workings of a poet's soul, which men will persist in calling "inspiration," had always had a charm for the Greeks, when he referred to Poe in the following words: "I need not remind you how deeply the young French poets of the romantic movement were stirred by Edgar Allan Poe's analysis of the working of his own imagination when he wrote that supremely imaginative work, 'The Raven.' "

Everybody is affected, according to Mr. Wilde, by sunrises and sunsets, but the absolute distinction of the artist is not so much in his capacity to feel as to interpret nature and the workings of the artistic spirit in the choice of subject. To the artist the present is not a whit more real than the past. For him no form is obsolete, no expression out of date; whether in the desert of Judea or the Arcadian valley; whether by the rivers of Troy or the rivers of Damascus; in the streets of the city or the byways of the country; he will take from his surroundings whatever is salutary for his own spirit, with the artistic control of one who is in the possession of the secret of beauty.

From the artist Mr. Wilde turned to the poet, and gave his audience his idea of poets. All things were not fit subjects for poetry—nothing that is harsh or disturbing; nothing that is debatable, or about which men argue. Calm and perfect repose were incarnate in Keats' "Ode to the Grecian

Urn," and the one dominant note in Morris' "Earthly Paradise," and in Burne-Jones' knights and ladies. To the poet all times and places are one. There is but one time—the artistic moment; one law—the law of form; one land—the land of beauty—"a land removed, indeed, from the real world, and yet more sensuous because more enduring; calm, yet with that calm which dwells in the faces of Greek statues." The wild-eyed sibyls and mighty-limbed prophets in the Sistine Chapel tell more of the real spirit of the Italian Renaissance, of the dream of Savonarola and the crime of Borgia, than the brawling boors and cooking women of Dutch art teach of the real spirit of the history of Holland.

Towards the close of his lecture Oscar told a little story of how he and others had endeavored to make a road across a swamp in order that some villagers might thereby be benefited. He did not say, however, whether knee-breeches were *au fait* on such occasions or not. He said that their enemies came and mocked them at their efforts. "We did not mind it much then, and do not mind it now at all. [Applause.] And so we worked for two months at our road. You ask, What became of that road? Well, that road ended like a bad lec-

ture—abruptly and in the midst of a swamp."
[Laughter.]

The young gentlemen whom Mr. Wilde met at
the german on Friday night were referred to as
"brilliant." This provoked great applause. He
liked their dancing, but they ought to cover the
naked pedestals of their characters with something
nobler. If they danced, he would rather they
danced minuets than polkas, for minuets had more
beauty. The city of Washington had a great
future in its sculpture. "You have got enough
now," he said, "to have more, but I don't think
you want any more bronze generals." [Laughter.]

He wanted the children to grow up in what
Plato called "the simple atmosphere of fair
things." The meanest vessel of the house could
awake the secret depths and longing of the soul.
It was in the nature of things that there should
always be hewers of wood and drawers of water,
but the pitcher at the well could, and should, be
a thing of beauty. Every object should be beautiful, and give delight to its maker as well as its
user, and lighten the burden of the toilers. For
those, the lecturer said, with whom the end of life
is not action but thought, "who must burn always
with one of the passions of this little, fiery-col-

ored world, and who, valuing passion for its intensity and not for its permanence, over and over again in the progress of their culture find what was once precious has become indifferent— for those who find life interesting not for its secrets but for its situations, for its pulsations and not for its purpose, the passion of beauty engendered by the decorative arts will be more satisfying than any political or religious enthusiasm, any enthusiasm for humanity, any ecstasy or sorrow of love, for art comes to you professing frankly to give nothing but the highest qualities to your moments as they pass."

Montreal Daily Witness, Monday, May 15, 1882.

OSCAR WILDE IN MONTREAL.

THE APOSTLE OF ART IN OUR MIDST—HIS APPEARANCE—WHAT HE HAS DONE AND WHERE HE HAS BEEN.

Few men, at least of his age, have been so much talked about, and certainly none so much laughed at, as Oscar Wilde. Curiosity as to his personal appearance has been by no means abated by the

many descriptions published, for readers at once
recognise the fact that in some cases the most vivid
language is useless to convey a correct impression,
and Oscar Wilde has been considered a sufficiently
unique personage to be one of those cases.   Consequently, when a *Witness* reporter was ushered into
the poet's room at the Windsor Hotel this morning, his personal as well as professional curiosity
was somewhat disappointed to find no poet visible.
He was there, however, and his apparent absence
was only due to the tobacco smoke which hovered
ethereally about his poetic form, and through
which his countenance was presently revealed. Re-
clining in an armchair in the midst of anything
but artistic, not to speak of æsthetic, surroundings
was the apostle of art and æstheticism.   Mr. Wilde,
as he rose and extended a large, gentle hand to the
visitor, showed to full advantage.   Tall, and well
proportioned, his large figure was clad in graceful
garments of soft homespun.   The absence of knee-
breeches and hose was at first a painful shock, but
the effect was partly removed by a glance at the
massive throat; the broad turned-down collar was
decidedly "all but," while the æsthetic dull red
necktie, baffling comprehension as to the manner
of its putting on, can only be described as "quite

consummately too." But attention could not remain long fixed on the attire. Mr. Wilde's face, surrounded and framed by a mass of long, untamed, tawny hair, is massive, almost colossal, and at the same time very pleasant in feature and expression, especially so far as the poetic eyes are concerned. But mere description, as was before hinted, is, of necessity, somewhat powerless.

Mr. Wilde, who speaks with the accent generally credited to the higher class of London society, and by no means uncommon in the region of Pall Mall, showed no objection whatever to being interviewed, and kindly refrained from making any of those unpleasant remarks about journalists which his experience with them would seem to justify. When asked what opinion he had formed of the probable results of his campaign, he at once said that after all the nonsense written about him had been forgotten, good and lasting results would remain. In the cities where he had been, decorative art societies had been started, and old societies had been brought into more prominence. His immense correspondence was entirely on this subject. "Here," said Mr. Wilde, "is a letter only received this morning, referring to the effect of my visit to Philadelphia last week." The letter was from

Charles Leland, the famous "Hans Breitmann," and a member of "the school," thanking Mr. Wilde for the good he had done in connection with the teaching of art principles to the young. These results are being seen in the increase of orders given to the art societies. Mr. Wilde mentioned an incident which showed the way in which he was able to help on native art. In Chicago he came across a young American sculptor of really extraordinary power and genius, but unknown. He spoke about him, and told the people that they could not really appreciate art if they neglected the native talent in their own city. Now that young sculptor has ever so many commissions.

The questioner asked how the British and Americans compared in their reception of his teachings. Mr. Wilde could hardly give a definite answer. "In America, you see, I have for the first time been face to face with people who have never seen any good art; as to their reception of what I say, while, no doubt, many come to hear me just from curiosity, yet afterwards I am continually getting letters from these people saying how they have been pleased with this or that point in my lectures. The great thing is to get them to come, for when they come they always see what I mean. And," said

Mr. Wilde, "what one really wants is not to be either blamed or praised, but to be understood."

"You have been all over the United States now, have you not, Mr. Wilde?"

"I have been all over the States except in the South, and I suppose, though it is difficult to guess, that I have spoken to some two hundred thousand people. I have found the people very willing and ready to listen and appreciate."

Mr. Wilde has been in California, and is quite enthusiastic over it. "It is Italy without art," was his judgment of the Hoodlum City. Only he objected to its being called the Hoodlum City. He said: "No, it is the city of fine men and beautiful women! San Francisco has the most lovely surroundings of any city except Naples I lectured there six times, and had the most delightful and appreciative audiences. People's appreciation of beauty depends so much on what they are accustomed to see around them. It might be thought otherwise from those who live in beautiful places not speaking about beauty, but they have no need to talk about it. That is our object. We want to see the homes of the people beautiful, and where this is the case people will no longer talk of the beautiful at all. We are forced to do so now because there are so many ugly things in the world. In the ideal state of art there will be no art lecturer."

Mr. Wilde went on to speak of the knowledge of art in the different countries, England and America. "In England, now, we have the great advantage of models of art always with us, in the cathedrals, in the colleges of Oxford and Cambridge, and in many buildings of the finest architecture. In America, the great want is of absolute models of art. The art which is learned from books is very worthless at best." Speaking of the aims of the movement with which he is identified, Mr. Wilde urged strongly that people should occupy a good deal more of their time with simple things. "It is all very well to devote time to little flower vases; they do for ladies' drawing-rooms; but that is not touching the people. It is the people we want to touch, and this can only be done by beginning with simple things. The least things, every household article, should be made beautiful, and I had far rather that, instead of designs for flower vases, a good design should be produced for a simple jug and basin, instead of the coarse pottery, inartistic in colour and outline, which is now common."

"What do you think is the present position of the movement in England, Mr. Wilde?"

"Well, you may best understand that from the fact that Mr. Morris has just received from Government the contract for the decoration of St. James's Palace. The movement is one that must be recognised. We have already altered the condition of society in respect to art, and no one will now furnish a house without having regard to art principles."

Mr. Wilde said all this with a simplicity of language and manner, and a hearty sincerity, which were quite refreshing after the caricatures which we have sometimes been led to imagine were imitations of the Arch-Æsthete. During the whole conversation "stained-glass" attitudes were conspicuously absent, and languid lackadaisicality was also entirely wanting. Once, indeed, the lithe-limbed poet sank into a position recalling in a faint degree certain creations of Du Maurier's imagination, and few could produce so æsthetic a yawn as once occurred in the intervals of puffing a cigarette. But these were evidently too natural to suggest even the ghost of a smile to the most risible. And when the visitor withdrew, leaving Oscar Wilde to plunge again into the wisdom of Mr. Shorthouse's

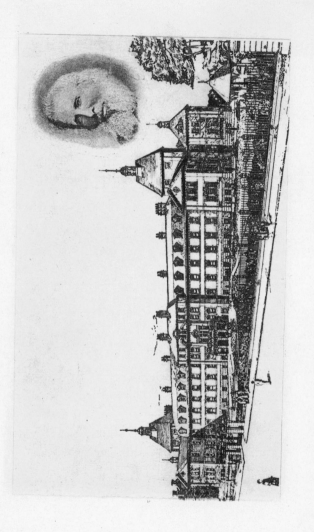

sudden-famed "John Inglesant," he thought as he went that behind the closed door there reclined neither a Postlethwaite, a Lambert Streyke, nor a Reginald Bunthorne, and that Messrs. Du Maurier, Burnand and Gilbert had all done him a grave injustice.

As an addendum to Colonel Morse's account of Wilde's American tour, the following items of the trip have interest:

Mr. Joaquin Miller wrote a letter in February of 1882 to Oscar Wilde, denouncing the "Philistine Press" of certain towns for its abuse of Wilde. Wilde wrote this reply to Miller:

MY DEAR JOAQUIN MILLER.

I thank you for your chivalrous and courteous letter to me, published in the *World*. Believe me, I would as lief judge of the strength and splendour of the sun and sea by the dusk that dances in the beam, and the bubble that breaks on the wave, as take the petty and profitless vulgarity of one or two insignificant towns as any test or standard of the real spirit of a sane, strong, and simple people, or allow it to affect my respect for the many noble men or women whom it has been my privilege in this great country to know.

For myself, and the cause which I represent, I have no fear as regards the future. Slander and folly have their way for a season, but for a season only, while as touching either the few provincial newspapers which have so vainly assailed me, or that ignorant and itinerant libeller, of New England, lecturing from village to village in such open and ostentatious isolation, be sure I have no time to waste on them! Youth being so glorious, art so godlike, and the very world about us so full of beautiful things, and things worthy of reverence, and things honourable, how should one stop to listen to the lucubrations of a literary gamin, to the brawling and mouthing of a man whose praise would be as insolent as his slander is impotent, or to the irresponsible and irrepressible chatter of the professionally unproductive? "'Tis a great advantage, I admit, to have done nothing, but one must not abuse even that advantage."

Who, after all, that I should write of him, is this scribbling anonymuncule in grand old Massachusetts, who scrawls and screams so glibly at what he cannot understand? This apostle of inhospitality, who delights to defile, to desecrate, and to defame the gracious courtesies he is unworthy to enjoy? Who are these scribes, who, passing with purposeless alacrity from the police news to the Parthenon, and from crime to criticism, sway with such serene incapacity the office which they so lately swept. "Narcissuses of imbecility," what should they see in the clear waters of Beauty and in the well undefiled of Truth, but the shifting and shadowy image of their own substantial stupidity?

Secure of that oblivion for which they toil so laboriously, and, I must acknowledge, with such success, let them peer at us through their telescopes and report what they like of us. But, my dear Joaquin, should we put them under the microscope there would be really nothing to be seen.

I look forward to passing another delightful evening with you on my return to New York, and I need not tell you that whenever you visit England you will be received with that courtesy with which it is our pleasure always to welcome all Americans, and that honour with which it is our privilege to greet all poets.

Most sincerely and affectionately yours,
OSCAR WILDE.

From the New York *Herald* is taken the following account of an amusing experience that Wilde had with bunco-steerers in December of 1882:

"As Oscar Wilde was walking up Broadway, he was accosted, near Union Square, by a hatchet-faced young man who introduced himself as a son of Mr. Drexel, the banker, of Drexel, Morgan & Co. He had seen the poet, he said, in his father's office, and took the liberty of making his acquaintance. Wilde had been in Mr. Drexel's office, and though he did not remember the junior Drexel, he expressed his pleasure at meeting him. The two went together to a restaurant, where Wilde's new-found friend developed quite an appetite. The poet remembered this with a grim smile when he was informed at police quarters later in the day that the man was known as 'Hungry Joe,' and was a noted bunco-steerer and confidence man.

"During the meal Mr. 'Drexel' incidentally mentioned that he had won a prize in a lottery, and suggested that Wilde go with him and get it. It was an old and worn bait, but the victim was innocent, and bit. He accompanied Mr. 'Drexel' to a house, whose number he could not afterward recall, and there found some men throwing dice. 'Drexel' threw once for Wilde, in fun, and won him quite a sum. Wilde was then induced to join the game. Soon he began to lose, and when a settlement was made found that he was sixty dollars out. Not having the ready money, he gave a cheque for the amount and played on. Soon he had lost a hundred dollars more, and he gave a cheque for that. Then once more he plunged into the game, and lost a thousand dollars. This brought Wilde to his senses, and while slowly signing the last cheque on the Madison Square Bank it came to his mind that he had been swindled, and he quickly formed a plan for getting the best of the swindlers. He arose to go, and shaking off Mr. 'Drexel,' who had risen to go with him, he called a cab as soon as he was out of the house and drove full speed to the Madison Square Bank and stopped payment on the three cheques which he had signed. The thieves doubtless followed him, and seeing where he went, they did not present the cheques. Having made sure of the money, Wilde visited the Thirtieth street police station and confessed his folly to Captain Williams. In the Rogues' Gallery he recognized his friend, Mr. 'Drexel' in the picture of 'Hungry Joe.' A few days later Captain Williams received the cheques by mail."

During his American visit Oscar Wilde was the subject of much social attention, both semi-public and private. In New York he was entertained at several private houses of people of social distinction, and he was tendered a reception at the Century Club; and in Philadelphia he also was considerably lionized and was the guest of honor at a reception given by the Saturday Club.

But perhaps the person whom Wilde most enjoyed meeting in Philadelphia's vicinage was the "good gray poet," Walt Whitman, whom he crossed the Delaware twice to visit in his Camden home.

On these visits Wilde was piloted by his American publisher, Mr. Joseph M. Stoddart, who has expressed his surprise, in a communication to the compiler of this biography, at the cordial and effusive greeting of welcome which Whitman accorded to the apostle of æstheticism, and the kindly and obviously sincere exchange of friendly words of appreciation from both men. This was a case indeed of extremes meeting, for certainly

the two men were at opposite poles in many respects.

During the visit, so Mr. Stoddart reports,
Wilde asked Whitman what method he adopted
in the writing of his poetry. "Well," answered
Whitman, "you know I was at one time of my
life a compositor and when a compositor gets to
the end of his stick he stops short and goes ahead
on the next line."

When Wilde first visited Whitman the latter
was living with his brother. Mrs. Whitman, the
poet's sister-in-law, in honor of the occasion produced a bottle of home-made wine distilled from
the elderberry. Wilde quaffed this not over-
palatable drink as if it were nectar of the gods.

After taking their leave, Mr. Stoddart suggested to Wilde that the drink must have been a
hard one for him to swallow. But Wilde answered
in a somewhat reproving way: "If it had been
vinegar I should have drunk it all the same, for
I have an admiration for that man which I can
hardly adequately express."

Of Whitman, Wilde has said: "If not a poet,
he is a man who sounds a strong note, perhaps
neither prose nor poetry, but something of his
own that is grand, original and unique."

Mr. Stoddart also piloted Wilde on an interesting call he made upon Father Maturin, rector of the Anglican Church of St. Clement in Philadelphia. Father Maturin was a cousin of Wilde's, and had sent an invitation to Wilde through Mr. Stoddart to "put him up," as the Father expressed it. The two Irish kinsmen appeared to enjoy the meeting greatly, but Wilde demurred to being "put up" when he had had a glimpse of the austere and somewhat meagre furnishings of an Anglican dormitory.

It was Mr. Stoddart, by the way, who published the much-discussed little volume of poems by Rennell Rodd, now Sir Rennell Rodd, entitled "Rose Leaf and Apple Leaf," and for which Oscar Wilde wrote an introduction, and a very fine and notable one. The "get-up" of the book, however, displeased Rodd so much that he would have nothing further to do with Wilde. Wilde had out of friendship for Rodd undertaken to find a publisher for an American edition of Rodd's first book of poems. The author was a young Oxford man at the time and not at all known on this side of the water.

Mr. Stoddart avers that Wilde was not altogether to blame for this rather remarkable product of the bookmaker's art, inasmuch as he himself somewhat in a spirit of humor designed the garb of the book. In the first place, Mr. Stoddart secured a small supply of some paper that had been made in the first paper mill in the United States, that of David Rittenhouse, and made either for bank-notes or bonds for the then new government of the United States. Of this lot there was only paper sufficient to print one hundred and seventy-five copies of the book.

Then the services of Mr. J. E. Kelly, the artist-sculptor, were secured to design some fantastic head and tail pieces, and the text was printed with mauve ink. The sheets were bound in vellum, and so the book emerged as a butterfly from its chrysalis state, probably the first "freak" book in America. This small edition, supposedly inspired as to its outward dress by the cult of the lily and the sunflower, was quickly bought up by collectors. Another and a cheaper and less ornate edition followed which met with a fair sale.

CHAPTER V.

FIRST SOJOURN IN PARIS.

On his return from America, Wilde made but a short stay in London, and then took up his residence in Paris in the spring of 1883, living at the Hotel Voltaire. He threw aside his mask and wig as an apostle of æsthetics, had his hair cut, and donned ordinary garments. Of his connection with the æsthetic movement he said: "That was the Oscar Wilde of the second period. I am now in my third period." It seemed as easy for Wilde to cast aside a pose as to affect one. He now indulged in humor at the expense of his apostleship, and delighted in recalling the humorous side of what he styled his "apostolic task," and of his American experiences, of which he told many amusing anecdotes.

Shortly after Wilde's arrival in Paris, Mr. Theodore Child, the correspondent of the London *World,* wrote to his paper as follows:

"Amongst other illustrious visitors to Paris, besides the Gladstone family, we have had, and still have, Oscar Wilde. Mr. Wilde is, of course, utterly unknown to the French, and does not probably intend to take any measures to make himself known. Last week he was entertained at dinner by some English and American artists and journalists, and at dessert he made a very clever little speech on his American experiences. Generally speaking, Mr. Wilde told us that while in America he had to converse on art with people who derived their notions of painting from chromo-lithographs, and their notions of sculpture from the figures in front of the tobacconists' shops. In Colorado, however, and the Rocky Mountains, Mr. Wilde was agreeably surprised by the æsthetic predisposition of the natives, and at Leadville, in particular, he found some of his own theories on art-police fully accepted. 'When I arrived in Leadville,' Mr. Wilde said, 'in the evening I went to the Casino. There I found the miners and pianist—sitting at a piano over which was this notice: "Please do not shoot at the pianist; he is doing his best." I was struck with this recognition of the fact that bad art merits the penalty of death, and I felt that in this remote city, where the æsthetic applications of the revolver were already admitted in the case of music, my apostolic task would be much simplified, as indeed it was.' "

Wilde delighted in the story of the pianist in Leadville, and it evidently went the rounds of Paris. In the diary of Edmund de Goncourt is this passage, dated May 5, 1883:

"Dined with the poet, Oscar Wilde. This poet, who tells the most improbable stories, gives us an amusing picture of a town in Texas, with its population of convicts, its revolver habits, its pleasure resorts, where one reads on a notice, 'Please not to shoot at the pianist, who is doing his best.' He tells us of the hall at the Casino, which, as it is the biggest room in the place, is used for the Assize Court, and here they hang criminals on the stage after the performance. He told us that he had seen there a man who had been hanged, clinging to the scenery uprights, while the audience fired revolvers at him from their seats.

"In those places, it would also appear, the theatrical managers look out for real criminals to play the parts of criminals, and when 'Macbeth' is to be staged and a person is wanted for the rôle of

Lady Macbeth, offers are made to a woman who has been convicted for poisoning, and who has just been released after serving her sentence. One sees posters thus worded: 'The part will be taken by Mrs. X.,' and, in brackets, the words 'ten years' penal servitude.'"

Here Wilde was evidently having fun with his audience by greatly exaggerating his experiences, or perhaps M. de Goncourt, who himself delighted to adorn a tale, is responsible for the extravagances in the anecdotes that he records.

Although Wilde had discarded his knee-breeches and silk stockings, he still was accredited with eccentricities of costume during his Parisian days, but there was method also in his eccentricity now. Sherard explains it thus:

"As a matter of fact, though Paris did not perceive it, Oscar Wilde was paying to French literature the compliment of modelling himself on the great writer, Balzac. He was then in a period of imitation of this great writer for whom his admiration increased with each year of his life. When at work at the Hotel Voltaire he used to put on a white gown with a monkish cowl, because it was in a dressing-gown like this that Balzac, who wrote mostly at nights, used to work. At the time when Balzac, who had doomed himself for years to celibacy and continence, at last went courting, the recluse assumed all the graces of the contemporary Parisian dandy. He wore the most elegant costumes, he adorned himself with jewellery, and he carried when he went abroad a walking-stick which was so noticeable that it inspired Delphine Gay with the subject of a novel, 'La Canne de Monsieur de Balzac.' In all these points Oscar Wilde imitated the master with whose industry and enthusiasm for literary art he was endeavouring to imbue himself. He dressed much after the fashion of the fops of 1848, he wore noticeable jewellery, and he carried a stick which was the replica of Balzac's *canne*. This was a stick of ivory with the pummel set with turquoises. The costume was the outward sign of a very laudable effort. It can be to nothing but the credit of any writer to wish to imitate Balzac; and if by adopting his peculiarities a man might hope to attain to any degree of his powers of production and style, one would like to see the whole Republic of Letters curled as to the hair, bejewelled, clad in 1848 costumes, and carrying ivory sticks with turquoise-stone pummels. But Paris did not understand the suggestion of Oscar Wilde's dress, and did not believe that a man who seemed to talk so flippantly had any real artistic strivings in him. Oscar forgot that not any more in Paris than in London, in London than in Berlin, are men prone to a charitable interpretation of any act of fellow man. He was labelled a *poseur* when he was only trying by dressing a part to enter into the very spirit of the man whom he wished to imitate in his excellent qualities."

Wilde soon became well known in Paris, and was well received in many quarters, numbering among his acquaintances Victor Hugo, Alphonse Daudet, Edmund de Goncourt, Sarah Bernhardt, Paul Bourget, and many of the leaders in artistic circles, especially of the impressionist school. A friend of Wilde's thus describes calling with him upon Sarah Bernhardt:

"I accompanied him on two occasions to Sarah Bernhardt, who showed great liking and admiration for him. On the first occasion we called on her at the Vaudeville Théâtre, during the performance of one of Sardou's plays, in which she was acting. We were received in the little salon adjoining her dressing-room, and Sarah, who was in evident dishabille, changing dresses for her part, put her head out between the dividing curtains to welcome Oscar Wilde with her most cordial smiles. Jean Richepin and other men were in the little drawing-room—the author of "Les Blasphèmes" with his arms folded—and it seems to me that our visit, no less than Sarah's evident pleasure in it, was somewhat resented.

"Some days later we went to her house on the Avenue de Villiers, and on the way Oscar Wilde purchased from a street hawker a large heap of wallflowers, which he presented to her. It was a poor offering, but she seemed delighted with it. We found Alexandre Parodi in her studio, who showed much deference to Oscar Wilde, and called him 'cher maitre.' Parodi was the author of that tragedy "Rome Vaincue," in which Sarah secured her first real stage triumph at the Comédie Française. I was much gratified by his attitude towards my new friend, for I knew Parodi's own worth; but Oscar Wilde found him rather tedious, and the fact was that Parodi, who had fallen on evil days, was very depressing in his conversation."

It was during his stay at the Hotel Voltaire that Wilde, under the influence of Poe, through Baudelaire, wrote one of his most striking and most pagan and sensual poems, "The Sphinx," and here also he wrote his play, "The Duchess of Padua," which some of his admirers have ranked with the masterpieces of the Elizabethan period. He wrote the play originally for Mary Anderson, and the manuscript was sent from Paris for her perusal. She declined it, however, much to the discomfiture of the author. But the actress showed good judgment in refusing the play, for despite its literary merits it proved to be not a good acting play. Lawrence Barrett finally accepted it, and brought it out under the name of "Guido Ferranti," in New York, during February, 1891. It ran but a week, and was withdrawn. The following notice of the play appeared in the New York *Herald* at the time, and is interesting, as it in part explains the reasons for the failure of the play:

"Mr. Oscar Wilde, the author of the tragedy of 'Guido Ferranti,' now running at the Broadway, may thank himself for the unflattering opinion of him held on this side of the Atlantic.

"It pleased him for some years to act the jester.

He donned the motley and he shook his bells. And people took him at his own cheap estimate. They smiled or scoffed. What wonder, then, if, as they looked back to his æsthetic freaks, some failed to see the real and serious merit of his play last week? We have been told, and the internal evidence appears to prove, that 'The Duchess of Padua' (as 'Guido Ferranti' was first called) was an early effort. It bears the marks of youthful power and honesty. It has a youthful warmth and youthful passion. It needs youthful actors to interpret it. And it appeals to youthful audiences.

"The talent it reveals is immature, and wild and imitative, like that of a well-read and gifted student. The fire which burns in every act is fierce, but, like the hero's, it is fickle and unsteady; it burns and it devours.

"I have read more than one queer comment on this 'Guido Ferranti.' Some kind, more cruel. The queerest view, I think, so far expressed in print, is that which damns it because it is 'so gloomy.' I never knew before that when a man wrote tragedies he was expected to make them light and sparkling.

"But it would seem I had a wrong idea of tragedy. It should be farcical, not sorrowful. Poor

Shakespeare blundered when he killed his Hamlet. Romeo should have lived on with Juliet. Macbeth should have turned monk and saved his soul.

"Well, if Mr. Wilde has erred he has erred well, and in good company. He did not dream that people clamored for farce-tragedy.

"His Guido and his Beatrice are not humorous. They are passionate and tragic. They die, in the last act, as Romeo died, and Juliet. The play, alas! is very, very gloomy. It is also very strong.

"The author is less happy in depicting character than in devising striking scenes and moving climaxes. The merit of the play is first dramatic, and only next is it poetical or psychological. The hero is an inconsistent soul. So, you may say, is Hamlet. Yes, but Hamlet explains his inconsistency, and Guido does not. He loves, he hates, he dares, he fears, he sins and he repents, as the wind blows, nor can we tell why he is changeable.

"Beatrice, his mistress, is more constant and intelligible. She has good grounds for loving, and then hating, and when she loves again she has a motive. Indeed, her very hate was love perverted —the love of a fond woman scorned and slighted.

"The play, as it stood when Mr. Wilde evolved it, was longer and more complex than the Barrett version. It was cut freely, and, on the whole, judiciously, to suit the stage. As it now stands it is a splendid and effective play, marred by some bombast and some plagiarisms, but saved by its intrinsic force and interest, and needing only better acting than Miss Gale's and Mr. Barrett's to make it a lasting and popular success."

Three years later a German translation of "The Duchess of Padua" was produced at one of the leading theatres of Hamburg, but here again the actors are reported as inadequate, and the play was withdrawn after a run of only three nights. The translation of the play by Dr. Max Meyerfeld, of Berlin, has been published, and is in every way an excellent one; it was reviewed in the *Daily Chronicle* by William Archer, who gave it great praise, and who hailed Oscar Wilde as a dramatic poet of very high rank.

Wilde lived quite luxuriously in Paris, and was often to be seen dining at the fashionable restaurants, at Bignon's in the Avenue de l'Opéra, the Café de Paris, or at Foyot's or Larenne's. At these cafés he met many literary people and artists. At the Café d'Orsay, where Wilde occasionally went, he was apt to run across Paul Bourget, with whom he struck up something of a friendship. But in those days Bourget was having a hard struggle and was depressed and reticent, while Wilde was exuberant and full of talk. Sherard, in his first book about Wilde, bearing the sub-title of "The Story of an Unhappy Friendship," thus describes a meeting between Wilde and Paul Verlaine:

"The two poets met at the Café François Premier, where Verlaine used to go for absinthe, and the distressful impression which poor Lelian of the satyr's face produced upon Oscar Wilde was such that he could not bear to meet him again. 'It was dreadful,' he said to me. Poor Lelian, by the way, carried off from this interview no other impression than that the English poet had an abundant stock of superior cigarettes, whilst he had to content himself with a penny screw of inferior tobacco. I suppose that all the brilliant things that Wilde said were lost upon the simple Verlaine, that child with the head of a Socrates, whose interests in life were reduced to their most material expression.

"He paid no heed to his brother poet's outpourings of eulogy. His little twinkling eyes leered now at the emptying glass and now at the silver cigarette case. His visitor, in his enthusiasm, forgot for once his natural hospitality."

But Wilde lived too extravagantly in Paris, for he had been producing but little. He spent the funds which had resulted from his American lecture tour, and also money that he received from the final disposal of some property in Ireland. Consequently he had to face the problem of earning a livelihood, and so returned to London in the spring of 1883. During August of this year he paid a second and a flying visit to the United States in order to look after the production of his play, "Vera, the Nihilist," which was produced for the first time on August 20, at the Union Square Theatre, with Miss Marie Prescott in the leading rôle. Previous to starting for America, Wilde wrote the two following interesting letters to Miss Prescott:

CHARLES STREET, GROSVENOR SQUARE, July, 1883.
MY DEAR MISS PRESCOTT:

It is with great pride and pleasure that I look forward to seeing you in the character of the heroine of my play—a character which I entrust to you with the most absolute confidence, for the first

night I saw you act I recognised in you a great
artist.

I do not only mean that there were strength and
splendour in your acting, music and melody in
your voice, and in every pose and gesture, as you
walked the stage, the infinite grace of perfect ex-
pressiveness, but that behind all these things,
which are merely the technique of acting, there
lay the true artistic nature which alone can conceive a part, and the true artistic power which
alone can create one.

As regards the play itself, I have tried in it to
express within the limits of art that Titan cry of
the peoples for liberty, which, in the Europe of
our day, is threatening thrones and making gov-
ernments unstable, from Spain to Russia, and from
north to southern seas. But it is a play not of politics, but of passion. It deals with no theories of
government, but with men and women simply; and
modern Nihilistic Russia, with all the terror of its
tyranny and the marvel of its martyrdoms, is
merely the fiery and fervent background in front
of which the persons of my dream live and love.
With this feeling was the play written, and with
this aim should the play be acted.

I have to thank you for the list of your company which you have sent me; and congratulate you, as well as myself, on the names of the many well-known and tried actors which I see it includes.

I am very much pleased to know that my directions as regards scenery and costume have been carried out. The yellow satin council chamber is sure to be a most artistic scene, and as you have been unable to match in New York the vermilion silk of which I sent you a pattern, I hope you will allow me to bring you over a piece large enough for your dress in the last act.

I look forward with much interest to a second visit to America, and to having the privilege of presenting to the American people *my first drama.* There is, I think, no country in the world where there are such appreciative theatrical audiences as I saw in the United States.

I hope that by the time I arrive the play will be in good rehearsing order, and I remain, dear Miss Prescott, your sincere friend and admirer,

OSCAR WILDE.

July, 1883.

MY DEAR MISS PRESCOTT:

I have received the American papers, and thank

you for sending them. I think we must remember that no amount of advertising will make a bad play succeed, if it is not a good play well acted. I mean that one might patrol the streets of New York with a procession of vermilion caravans twice a day for six months to announce that "Vera" was a great play, but if on the first night of its production the play was not a strong play, well acted, well mounted, all the advertisements in the world would avail nothing. My name signed to a play will excite some interest in London and America. Your name as the heroine carries great weight with it. What we want to do is to have *all* the real conditions of success in our hands. Success is a science; if you have the conditions, you get the result. Art is the mathematical result of the emotional desire for beauty. If it is not thought out, it is nothing.

As regards dialogue, you can produce tragic effects by introducing comedy. A laugh in the audience does not destroy terror, but, by relieving terror, aids it. Never be afraid that by raising a laugh you destroy tragedy. On the contrary, you intensify it. The canons of art depend on what they appeal to. Painting appeals to the eye, and is founded on the science of optics. Music appeals to the ear and is founded on the science of acoustics. The drama appeals to human nature, and must have as its ultimate basis the science of psychology and physiology. Now, one of the facts of physiology is the desire of any intensified emotion to be relieved by some emotion that is its opposite. Nature's example of the dramatic effect is the laughter of hysteria or the tears of joy. So, I cannot cut out my comedy lines. Besides, the essence of good dialogue is interruption. All good dialogue should give the effect of its being made by the reaction of the personages on one another. It should never seem to be ready-made by the author, and interruptions have not only their artistic effect but their physical value. They give the actors time to breathe and get new breath power.

I remain, dear Miss Prescott, your sincere friend,

OSCAR WILDE.

Upon his arrival in New York for the second time, Wilde was interviewed by a *Herald* reporter, who seemed to wonder at Wilde's change of appearance.

"I see you have had your hair cut," observed the reporter.

"Oh, yes," said the poet. "To the amazement of Europe, I cut off my locks. I never had my hair cut in my life until last March."

"How did it happen?"

"It's rather interesting, I think. You see, I was in the gallery of the Louvre, in Paris, and I saw a bust of a young Roman Emperor. It was very beautiful indeed. As soon as I saw that the young emperor had his hair cut short, I wanted to be like him."

"Are you?"

"So far as the hair is concerned, I think I am. I got a hairdresser—and the French hair-dressers are artists—to come with me to the Louvre, and I showed him the young emperor's bust. He cut my hair after the fashion he saw there—as nearly as he could. I afterwards found that the bust represented Nero, one of the worst behaved young men in the world, and yet a man of strong artistic passion. I thought it just suited my case. Speaking of my hair, the truth is that people mistake the forms of art for the principle. There is only one principle in art, and yet millions of forms. The majority of people think that one cannot admire art unless one's hair falls below one's collar. I want to show them that they are mistaken. I wore my hair long because I think that long hair is beautiful when it is properly cut."

"You have given up knee-breeches?"

"For the present, yes. You see, one's taste changes; and besides, one must suit one's trousers to the cut of one's hair. I think there is really a strong desire among young men to wear knee-breeches, but it requires great courage to begin. But they were invented for a period when men wore wigs. We cannot wear short breeches and short hair. That would be absurd."

"Vera, the Nihilist," was produced, as has been said, on August 20. It was under the management of Mr. W. Perzel, the husband of Marie Prescott, the leading lady. The entire cast was as follows:

VERA, THE NIHILIST.

The Palace.

The Czar..............Mr. George C. Boniface
Prime Minister..............Mr. Edward Lamb
Baron Roff.................Mr. James Wright
Prince Petrovitch...........Mr. William Wilson

Count Rouvaloff............Mr. John F. De Gez
Marquis De Poivrard..........Mr. Charles Day
General Ketemkin........Mr. George S. Paxton
Colonel of the Guard......Mr. Thomas Brunick
Page.......................Mr. Louis Mann

The People.

Peter Savoureff, an innkeeper...Mr. Julius Kahn
Demitri, his son............Mr. Frederick Lotto
Vera, his daughter.........Miss Marie Prescott
Michael, a peasant..........Mr. B. W. Turner
Alexis, a medical student....Mr. Lewis Morrison
Nicholas, a child.............Frankie Furlong
President of the Nihilists......Mr. J. R. Furlong
Professor Marfa.........Mr. Edward Harding

In spite of careful preparation and a lavish expenditure of money for costumes and scenery, the play was a total failure. It was withdrawn after but one week's run. It was severely criticised by the New York papers, and Miss Prescott took up the cudgels herself against the critics, whom she denounced in a published letter, insinuating that their attitude was one of preconcerted condemnation.

"Vera" was Wilde's first attempt at playwriting. It has been asserted that he wrote the play as early as 1876. After its failure in New York he returned immediately to London. Here he had already met his former lecture manager in America, Col. W. F. Morse, and had made arrangements with him for a second lecture tour beginning in London and extending to the provincial towns. In the succeeding chapter Colonel Morse will tell in his own words the details of this second lecture tour.

CHAPTER VI.

LECTURES IN GREAT BRITAIN.

By W. F. Morse.

In the spring of 1883 the writer was in London as the representative of an American publishing house, which was about to bring out an important book of which it was thought desirable to publish a special English edition.

Mr. Wilde had come from Paris, where he had been since returning from America, having found it necessary to earn money for his current expenses. He called at my office, about the middle of June, and there was then arranged a preliminary lecture in London, to be followed by others throughout the country should the results of this first effort prove satisfactory.

The preliminary announcements were simply that Mr. Wilde would speak at Princes' Hall, Piccadilly, on July 9, giving his "Personal Impressions of America."

The arrangements at Princes' Hall on the night of the lecture were, as nearly as possible, the same as those at Chickering Hall on his first appearance in New York, except that there was no introduction of the speaker. A large audience was present, drawn perhaps by curious motives, and included many Americans, who were dubious as to what might be said touching the American lack of appreciation of the artistic ideas of the speaker.

On Mr. Wilde's appearance there was an evident disappointment because of the omission of the peculiar costume which he had worn at his public addresses in America. There was a slight recognition of Mr. Wilde's presence as he made his bow to the audience, but neither then nor thereafter was there any prolonged applause.

On the day after the lecture the following account of it appeared in the London *World:*

"The curiously expectant folk who went out to Princes' Hall 'for to see' the typical æsthete were somewhat pleasantly surprised to find a very sensible and observant young man, who touched on a vast variety of transatlantic subjects with decided originality, somewhat audacious brilliancy, and a good deal of quaintly quiet humour. Mr. Oscar

Wilde's method of lecturing has somewhat puzzled the critics who date from the time of Albert Smith, and the discourse was a sort of subtle philosophical all-round chat, sometimes extravagantly coloured, sometimes fanciful, vague in structure, and full of a strong personal interest and an undercurrent of Irish fun. It was a decidedly new method of approaching life, and travellers may take an odd hint or two from Oscar's curiously amusing fashion of making a vivid sketch-book of the men and women, and mountains, and rivers, and theatres, and tea-cups, and magnolias, and moons, and girls, that he drifted across in his picturesque 'pilgrim's progress.' I thought the lecture was a little too long, the stories excellently told, the voice clear and quiet, the paradoxes a little too subtle for the audience, and the whole thing original, and quaint, and interesting."

The *Queen* said:

"Paradoxical, audacious, epigrammatic, abounding in good stories well told, in picturesque descriptions, often humorously nonsensical, with plenty of original information."

This introduction of Mr. Wilde to a London audience was deemed sufficient to warrant his presentation throughout the English provinces.

At that time there was no regular system for placing lectures or making up a connected tour of engagements. The Mechanics' or Literary Institutes of the United Kingdom were usually the agencies by which speakers came into contact with the public, and these were accustomed to provide practical subjects, topics of real every-day interest, or a form of entertainment in magic and legerdemain, dialect monologues, illustrated travels, or musical comedies and concerts. The lectures of Mr. Wilde took their place on the list, and were a part of the series, except in one or two of the larger cities, where they were managed as in this country, for the joint benefit of the theatre and speaker.

Up to January, 1884, he had spoken upwards of sixty-six times in England and Scotland, and had prepared a new lecture, "The Value of Art in Modern Life."

He had also a special talk for art schools, delivered first before the students of the Royal Academy, London, upon "Modern Art Training."

Some of the biographers of Mr. Wilde have

taken exception to the style and manner in which he was sometimes announced or advertised, claiming that it was made clear to him that "his success was expected not from the value and interest of the address, but from the notoriety attaching to his name as the eccentric æsthete."

In support of this is quoted the vulgarity of a displayed advertisement: "He is coming! Oscar Wilde, the Great Æsthete!"

It is possible there may have been instances of this kind when Mr. Wilde's reputation as an æsthete was put before the man's acknowledged powers as a speaker, but this was due to the local managers, and was not done with the consent of his agents, and was always to the distaste of Mr. Wilde himself.

The announcements sent out under my management were little pamphlets giving a sketch of the lecturer's life and an account of his writings, extracts from press notices of the lectures which appeared in America and England, and the following abstracts of the two lectures, "The House Beautiful," and "Personal Impressions of America":

"The lecture, 'The House Beautiful,' is, for the most part, an exposition of the application of the principles of true artistic decoration to the exterior and interior of the homes of the people. He takes up in detail each one of the elements that enter into the complete artistic furnishing of a room, and gives elaborate schemes of colour and art decoration which properly supplement each other. He points out the defects and inconsistencies which, under our present style, produces in many cases a sense of discord and inharmoniousness, not easy to define, but which, if once brought to notice, can always hereafter be avoided.

"Mr. Wilde will also offer some observations upon style and colour in dress for the house and in the street: on the influence of artistic surroundings upon children: and on the value of handicrafts as the basis of education. The lecture will contain the principal portion of the address delivered by Mr. Wilde during his late American tour, together with much additional matter relative to the present position and future development of art decoration in this country.

"The lecture, 'Personal Impressions of America,' will include many topics suggested by his personal experiences; the methods, advantages, and annoyances of railway travelling; the varied phases of American life and character, as seen under all sorts of conditions, pleasant and otherwise; the distinctive architecture and public works of the country; the position, development, and prospects of art in all its various forms; the status, education, and training of women; their influence, and their theories of dress; the journalism of the United States—with incidental remarks upon the peculiar methods of interviewing as applied to himself; a sketch of distinctive classes and communities—the Miners of Colorado, the Mormons of Salt Lake, the Chinese of San Francisco, and the Indians of the Plains; the amusements of the people, the theatres and actors, and the athletic sports; closing with some observations upon the educational facilities offered to every class, and the influence of these advantages upon the business, social and political character of the American people."

During the season of 1883-84 Mr. Wilde delivered upwards of one hundred and fifty addresses in all parts of the United Kingdom. He had no travelling agent or manager except at places where a lecture was arranged for independently of the local managers and associations. As a rule, these were the most successful ones of the season, rarely failing to attract large and appreciative audiences.

Undoubtedly there is a wide difference between the average English and American lecture audiences in many ways which are obvious to the speaker and to the manager as well. One thing was noticeable—there were no recalls, no second lectures. The audiences were satisfied with one appearance, and the speaker had to accept the verdict of the public.

The lectures were to Mr. Wilde a means of livelihood. He disliked the railway journeys and the hotel life, and these wore upon him; and while lecturing itself was not distasteful to him, yet he naturally grew weary of the constant repetition, the telling of the same stories and anecdotes night after night. The returns from this series of lectures, while of considerable consequence, were not as large as those in America, for the English scale of compensation to public speakers is not up to the American standard. However, the amount that Mr. Wilde received was sufficient to provide for his immediate future and to enable him to carry out certain plans that he had formed.

With the close of the season of 1884 my association with Mr. Wilde as manager for his lectures terminated, though he still continued to lecture intermittently for two years longer under the management of a London lecture agency.

———

A few extracts from the notices of the provincial papers will give an idea of how Oscar Wilde's lectures were received in the provinces:

"May be characterised as a 'discursive' record of the impressions created in the mind of a keen observer of a country in which there is so much that strikes an Englishman as at once strange and interesting."—*Southport Visitor.*

"The appearance of Mr. Oscar Wilde at the Gaiety Theatre in his native city attracted a large audience. It was an audience that came out of compliment to the lecturer and sympathy with the art principle which he is popularly understood pre-eminently to represent.—*Dublin Correspondence.*

"Mr. Wilde's narrative of his experiences during nearly a year's travel over the great continent was cheerfully discursive, and evidently gave great entertainment to his audience, who for two hours

were interested and amused with a discourse largely anecdotal and abounding in touches of lively
humour. The lecturer was warmly received on
stepping on to the platform, and the favourable
impression created by his opening remarks was sustained to the end. Mr. Wilde is to be congratu-
lated on his ability to take a comprehensive grasp
of the subjects brought under his notice, and a
cheerful cosmopolitanism which made him a general favourite wherever he went."—*Globe.*

"The lecture was pleasing, and the words were
at times eloquent and well chosen. They were delivered in a pleasing voice, with easy manner, and
without any attempt at attitudinising or dramatic
effect; the elocution was appropriate. On the
whole, it was a highly agreeable lecture, from a
pleasing and cultivated source."—*England.*

Following is a pen picture drawn of Wilde by
a provincial journalist, rather vulgar in style, but
interesting as showing the provincial idea of one
evidently still regarded as the high priest of æstheticism:

"Oscar Wilde, the æsthetic—the ineffable—the exponent of the principle of eternal loveliness—has visited us and is—*human*. He is not an angel, after all. Nor is he a deity springing to us out of the dark past. His food must have been other than the nectar'd sweets the poets love to write about; in fact, he can be seen, and heard, and handled, for he is a—man. This revelation will come as an unwelcome surprise to many. One so delightfully out of sympathy with the age, with such ineffable yearnings towards the romantic past, with such inexpressible aspirations towards the beauteous future, when the essential ugliness of to-day shall only be remembered as a hideous dream, such a man cannot be—ought not to be—one of us. So I am sure many think. I believe it was Mrs. Browning who describes how sad we feel when we find our cherished idols simply to be clay; but I can confess to no such revelation of feeling when Mr. Oscar Wilde stepped on to the platform and I discovered he had no wings. Mr. Oscar Wilde is tall, well proportioned, with a poet's hair, and—shall I say it—a mildly epicurean countenance. In his appearance there was nothing Byronic, or Bulwerian, or Carlylean, or Ruskinesque; a little that savoured of Count d'Orsay, Beau Brummel, and more that suggested the traditional diner-out. His dress had few peculiarities, being ordinary evening dress, a very wilderness of shirt-front, relieved by a half-concealed scarlet handkerchief, deftly placed inside his vest. His pose and manner might have been artistic, but were not particularly effective. His voice is a moderately pleasing one, with an occasional lisp to give it an aristocratic tone. His action—what little there was of it—was striking. He spoke entirely extempore, not even availing himself of the use of notes. For very much more than an hour he addressed his audience. There was no hesitation and there was no fire. Only once there was an approach to pathos, and, as far as I could detect, only one quotation from the poets, excepting an extract he gave in the form of a letter—I think— of John Keats. He came to speak to us on an important subject. And here I must say that if his lecture had been called the 'Home Beautiful,' instead of the 'House Beautiful,' I should have been better pleased. Englishmen—especially such as would go and hear such a discourse as Oscar Wilde's—do not care much for their 'houses,' they care everything for their homes. An Englishman never says he is going to his 'house,' but always

that he is going 'home.' A house, to an Englishman, is an empty building. The same building
filled with furniture, and all sorts of lovely things
—plus wife and children—becomes a home."

Upon people of refinement generally through the
provinces Wilde seems to have produced a strong
and lasting impression. A lady from one of the
Midland towns, long after the lecture tour, thus
writes of the impression made upon her by the
lecturer:

"I can remember him as though I had seen him
yesterday. My mother was delighted with his appearance; she often afterward spoke of his hair
and his hands and his tie—oh! his tie, how it
impressed us all. For my part, though I was only
a girl then, I felt he was saying things which nobody present could understand, and it seemed to
me at times as though he knew it also. I felt it
was a pity he should have had to come here at
all, for I suppose it was necessity that drove him on
to the lecture platform. Many of the things he said
have remained familiar to my mind ever since.
I never see a big curtain-pole without thinking
of what he said about the sins of the upholsterer,

and I know that I never drink a cup of tea at a railway refreshment room without remembering how he described the cup out of which he drank his coffee at the hotel in San Francisco, where he contrasted the crockery of the Chinese in the Chinese quarter of that city with the domestic vessels used by the Europeans. It was a real distress to me to sit in that lecture-room, looking at this wonderful youth, and listening to his profound and beautiful words, while the rest of the audience were either gazing with dismay and surprise, or showing how bored they were. The room was not half full, to begin with, and during the whole course of the lecture people kept getting up and going out. But he seemed quite indifferent to the mood of his audience; his manner, if I may use the term in such a connection, was quite business-like. It was as if he was saying to himself, 'I am here to say certain things, and I shall go on speaking until I have said them.' He began speaking the moment he came on the stage, and when he had said his last word he walked off as if anxious to catch a train and get away from us all."

CHAPTER VII.

MARRIAGE.

Women generally appear to have been much impressed with Wilde's lectures, and during this tour, and while lecturing in Dublin, he won a charming and beautiful wife, Miss Constance Lloyd, of that city, who was also an heiress. The marriage took place on May 29, 1884. Mr. Edmund Yates published this notice of the event in the *World:*

"Mr. Oscar Wilde's wedding went off with more simple effect than the large crowd who thronged the church had possibly come out to see. Owing to the illness of Mr. John Horatio Lloyd, the bride's grandfather, the ceremony was meant to be of rather a private character, and only the near relatives were asked to meet at Lancaster Gate after the service. There is only this much to be recorded about it: that the bride, accompanied by her six pretty bridesmaids, looked charming; that Oscar bore himself with calm dignity; and that all most intimately concerned in the affair seemed thoroughly pleased. A happy little group of *intimes* saw them off at Charing Cross."

On the day of the wedding the young couple started for Paris, and there spent their honeymoon. On their return to London they leased a comfortable mansion in Tite Street, No. 16, Chelsea. It was substantially furnished, and was decorated under the direction of Whistler. This was the home of the Wildes until came the tragedy and separation.

The period of the honeymoon in Paris seems to have been a radiantly happy one, and Oscar Wilde renewed many of his old acquaintances and made many new ones. Among the latter was M. Jean Joseph-Renaud, who later translated into French Wilde's "Intentions." Renaud first met Wilde at the house of some of Mrs. Wilde's relations in Paris, and in his preface to his translation of "Intentions" he writes thus of this meeting:

"When an hour late, Mr. Wilde entered the drawing-room, we saw a tall gentleman, who was

too stout, who was clean-shaven, and who differed
from any Auteuil bookmaker, by clothes in better
taste than a bookmaker wears, by a voice which
was exquisitely musical, and by the pure blue
light, almost like that of a child's eyes, which
shone in his look.   In his bulky cravat of green-
ish silk an amethyst sparkled with a subdued light;
his grey gloves, which were so fine as to be almost
transparent, moulded his graceful hands; an orchid
was shrivelling itself up in his button-hole.   Without listening to the names of the people who
were introduced to him he sat down, and with an
air of exhaustion begged Madame Lloyd to order
the shutters of the dining-room to be closed and
candles to be lighted.   He said that he could not
possibly stand the light of day.   .   .   .

"The table decorations had to be altered. because the mauve flowers would have brought him
bad luck.   Then, as soon as the *hors d'œuvres* had
been served he took definite possession of the
conversation.   What a disappointment awaited
us!   He spoke 'pretentiously,' asked questions, and
did not wait for the replies, or addressed himself
to people with too great directness.   'You have
never seen a ghost?   No!   Oh!   Now you,
Madame, yes, you, Madame, your eyes seem to

have contemplated ghosts. . . .' Then he declared that one night in a bar each table was put in its place, and the floor was swept, not by waiters, but by 'the angels of the close of the day.' His British accent reminded us of Sarah Bernhardt. . . . He next began to tell us, speaking almost in whispers, as though he were telling us secrets, and using mysterious phrases, some poetical and simple tales . . . about a young fisherman who pretends every night as he returns from the sea to have seen syrens; one day he really does see a syren, but when he comes home he does not say so . . . about a sculptor who with the bronze of a statue of 'Pain Which Lives Forever' moulds the statue of 'Pleasure Which Lasts but for One Moment.' Next he returned to what was *macabre,* and described at length the sensations which a visit to the Morgue in the different capitals of the world procures to a man. We found in M. Wilde the hoaxing cynicism of Baudelaire and Villiers de l'Isle-Adam as it appeared through an English medium. Already that fashion of amazing people seemed much out of date, and to this audience of intelligent *bourgeois* it was successful only in the bad sense of the word. The poet noticed this. He kept silent during the rest of

the meal.   But later on in the drawing-room,
while coffee was being served, the conversation
having turned on the success of a French comedy
in England and Germany, he gently suggested
that our prodigious theatrical instinct explains
many of our acts: French foreign politics, for
instance, are theatrical; they aim rather at the
finest attitude, the most striking phrases, the most
effective gestures, than at any practical successes.
He then examined our history at length, from
Charles X up to modern times, from a paradoxical
point of view.   His conversation transformed itself; he displayed extraordinary knowledge and
wit.   Men, deeds, treaties, wars passed under review with appreciations, unsuspected, amusing,
exact.   He made them glitter under the light
of his words, even as a jeweller awakes new lights
in his gems.

"He then went on to talk about Lady Bless-
ington and Disraeli.

"To tell us of the pains of love of Lady Bless-
ington he little by little raised himself to a lofty
and intoxicating lyricism; his fine voice hymned,
grew tender, rang out, like a viol, in the midst of
the emotional silence.   This Englishman, who
just before had appeared grotesque, reached,

reached with simplicity, aye, surpassed, the expressive power of the most admirable odes of humanity. Many of us were moved to tears. One had never thought that the words of man could attain to such splendour. And this took place in a drawing-room, and the man who was speaking never spoke otherwise than as a man speaks in a drawing-room. We could understand that a great lady had said of him: 'When he is speaking I see round his head a luminous aureole.' "

This remark was made by a lady to Henri de Régnier, the poet, essayist and novelist. He also in his book of essays, "Figures et Caractères," pays a tribute to the impression which Wilde at this period made in Paris. He describes the dinner at which the lady referred to made the remark quoted by Renaud:

"The dinner, elegant and prolonged, was held in a luxurious room, brilliantly lighted. Scented violets were banked upon the cloth. In the cut-crystal glasses champagne sparkled; fruits were being peeled with knives of gold. M. Wilde was speaking. There had been invited to meet him certain guests who were not talkative, and who were disposed to listen to him with pleasure. Of this conversation and of others I have kept a vivacious and lasting remembrance. M. Wilde spoke in French with an eloquence and a tact which were far from common. His expressions were embellished with words which had been most judiciously selected. As a scholar of Oxford, M. Wilde could as easily have employed Latin or Greek. He loved the Greek and Roman antiquities. His *causerie* was all purely imaginative. He was an incomparable teller of tales; he knew thousands of stories which linked themselves one to the other in an endless chain. . . .

"One might not press M. Wilde too closely for the meaning of his allegories. One had to enjoy their grace and the unexpected turns he gave to his narratives, without seeking to raise the veil of this phantasmagoria of the mind which made of his conversation a kind of 'Thousand and One Nights' as spoken.

"The gold-tipped cigarette went out and lighted itself again incessantly in the lips of the story-teller. As his hand moved with a slow gesture the *scarabæus* of his ring threw off its green lights. The face kept changing its expression with the most amusing mimicry; the voice flowed on unceasingly, dragging a little, always equal.

"M. Wilde was persuasive and astonishing. He excelled in giving a certificate of truth to what was improbable. The most doubtful statement when uttered by him assumed for the moment the aspect of indisputable truth. Of fable he made a thing which had happened actually; from a thing which had actually happened he drew out a fable. He listened to the *Schéhérazade* that was prompting him from within, and seemed himself first of all to be amazed at his strange and fabulous inventions. This particular gift made of M. Wilde's conversation something very distinct amongst contemporary *causeries*. It did not, for instance, resemble the profound and precise ingenuity of M. Stéphane Mallarmé, which explained facts and things in a manner so delicate and exact. It had nothing of the varied, anecdotic talk of M. Alphonse Daudet with his striking *aperçus* on men and things. Nor did it resemble in any way the paradoxical beauty of the sayings of M. Paul Adam, or the biting acridity of M. Henri Becque. M. Wilde used to tell his stories like Villiers de l'Isle-Adam told them. . . . M. Wilde charmed and amused, and he gave one the impression that he was a happy man at ease in life."

Elsewhere de Régnier says: "He pleased, he amused, he astounded. People grew enthusiastic about him; people were fanatics where he was concerned. Indeed, all who came into close contact with Wilde bear testimony to the extraordinary brilliancy of his conversation. Speaking of the Irish, Wilde himself once said: 'We are too poetical to be poets. We are a nation of brilliant failures, but we are the greatest talkers since the Greeks.'"

When Wilde with his young bride returned to London he turned to journalism as a means of livelihood and occasionally appeared on the lecture platform. His wife's income at that time was not large and it was not until the death of her grandfather, which occurred much later, that she came into a fortune. Wilde contributed much anonymous work to *The World* and *The Pall Mall Gazette,* but this was mostly of a pot-boiling kind. But also at this time he was writing the beautiful tales which were republished in a volume in 1888, "The Happy Prince and Other Tales," and which certainly rank among the very best fairy tales ever told in the English language, or for that matter in any language.

In June, 1885, a son, named Vivian, was born to the Wildes, and another son, Clarence, was born in November, 1886. These added responsibilities made Oscar Wilde all the more anxious to increase his income, and in October, 1887, he accepted the editorship of a fashion journal called *The Woman's World,* published by Cassell & Co., and this position he held for two years.

By all accounts Wilde proved himself to be a very painstaking and competent editor. He contributed each month a department occupying about five pages of the periodical and dealing with literary matters entitled "Literary and Other Notes." It is a pity that these really brilliant essays on contemporary literature did not have a better and worthier setting. Apart from his editorial work he still continued to contribute articles to the daily and weekly press and to magazines. Later, after he had turned his back on Fleet Street, he appears to have conceived a great detestation of journalism. In his remarkable essay, "The Soul of Man Under Socialism," published in 1891, there occurs this scathing sentence: "In centuries before ours the public nailed the ears of journalists to the pump. That was quite hideous. In this century journalists have nailed their own ears to the keyhole. This is much worse." In many of his plays Wilde also has other flings at the press. It is hardly to be wondered at that the press often had its fling at him.

A picture of the happy domestic life of Oscar Wilde is given by Mrs. Frank Leslie, who married "Willie" Wilde and subsequently divorced him. In an interview in 1895, she spoke thus of Oscar Wilde's wife and his home life in London:

"I want to tell you about Oscar Wilde's wife. She is an Irishwoman and was a Miss Constance Lloyd. She inherited a large sum of money on the death of her father, who had great shipping interests. She is the prettiest, daintiest, most graceful woman you ever saw, and after eleven years of married life she still adores her husband. While his dress is now strictly conventional, she continues to affect the æsthetic in all her costumes. Why, she's the purest, simplest thing. She wouldn't even tell a society fib. She's as cold as marble, but through the ice you can see the warm glimmer of heartfelt admiration for her husband. Her reception days are Wednesdays, and a marvellous feature of them is the invariable presence of her husband. He always stays at home on her reception days—a remarkable thing, I think, after eleven years of wedded life. It is beautiful to observe how she is always looking up to him, always appealing for his approval in everything she says.

"Their home in Tite Street, Chelsea, is a marvel of well-ordered appointment and elegant taste. The drawing-room is decorated in white and gold, but the furniture reproduces in its models and combinations the 'greenery-yallery' effect. Some of the finest water-colors I ever saw adorn the walls. And then the persons you meet there are the wittiest and brainiest in London. There you will see Swinburne, ever an intimate and admirer of Oscar Wilde; and Whistler, who got off that famous joke which set the whole literary world laughing and wagging its head. It happened at a dinner party. Whistler had said something remarkably clever, and Wilde remarked, 'I wish to heavens, Whistler, I'd said that myself.' To which the artist responded, 'You will, Oscar. You will, in time.'

"Oscar Wilde's boys are Vivian and Clarence. They are splendid fellows, with the mop of Wilde hair growing low over their foreheads.   This Wilde hair is a marvel.   It keeps the members of this remarkable family in the realm of perpetual youth. Even at her advanced age, it covers, when released, the shoulders of Lady Wilde like a thick veil.

"But let me tell you about these boys.   They have been most carefully nurtured.   Oscar's fad has been that they should never go to school until they were thoroughly robust physically.   The consequence is that their education has been directed, so far, exclusively by the father and mother.   Mr. Wilde would never have a tutor in his house, or indeed, for that matter, a male servant of any description.   It is a noticeable fact that at all his great dinners Mr. Wilde's guests are always served by women waiters.

"These boys are such perfect gentlemen.   Their home life is so well ordered.   I remember on one occasion asking Vivian whether he had been to see a certain one of his father's plays.   His reply was so astounding that I have never forgotten it.   'No,' he said, 'there are certain epigrams in that play which mamma doesn't think it fit for me to hear.' "

Mrs. Leslie goes on to speak of Oscar Wilde's great affection for his sons and for his mother, and of her own long and unbroken friendship with the Wildes.

It was after his connection with *The Woman's World* that the writings of Wilde began to attract a more universal attention than had heretofore been given them. His remarkable essay, "The Soul of Man Under Socialism," appeared in *The Fortnightly Review* in February, 1891; it produced a profound impression upon the Continent and has been translated into almost every tongue. At about this time Wilde published several books which commanded wide attention: "A House of Pomegranates"; "The Happy Prince and Other Tales"; "The Picture of Dorian Gray"; and "Intentions," a collection of essays. Sherard quotes "a man of the very highest scholarship and learning in England," as thus expressing himself after reading "Intentions": "I seemed to see the meaning of literature and art as I never had before; in fact he (Wilde) taught me the secret I had always missed. I said: 'Never man spoke like this man!' It was a revelation; more so than when I read Plato. I secured all his books I could. Every friend of mine with any culture or insight seems to have the same experience on reading him."

In the London *Academy* of July 4, 1891, Mr.
Richard Le Gallienne thus reviews "Intentions,"
then but recently published:

Mr. Wilde, in speaking of the methods open
to the critic, well says that Mr. Pater's narrative is, of course, only criticism in disguise: his
figures are but personifications of certain moods
of mind, in which he is for the time interested,
and which he desires to express. Now I have
been wondering whether one should not similarly
regard Mr. Wilde essentially as a humourist who
had taken art criticism for his medium, just as
Carlyle was a humourist in the odd disguise of a
prophet. Certainly, I am inclined to think that
much of his intricate tracery of thought and
elaborate jewel-work of expression is simply built
up to make a casket for one or two clever home-
less paradoxes.   "The fact of a man being a
poisoner is nothing against his prose." Mr. Wilde
somehow struck that out, and saw that it was
deserving of a better fate than to remain a waif
of traditionary epigram; so he went to work on
Lamb's strange friend, Thomas Griffiths Wainewright, one of the subtlest art critics and poisoners
of his time, unearthed his curious history, made

selections from his criticisms, and then set his own epigram, diamond-wise, in the midst of a biographical essay. Various readers solemnly add to their historical knowledge, discuss the strange character of the man, study his criticism; but Mr. Wilde sits and watches his epigram sparkling far within. About Wainewright he cares far less than the reader; about his own epigram, far more.

Of course this is not the whole truth about these "Intentions"; the whole truth is a many-coloured thing about a personality so complex as that of the author of "Dorian Gray." But it is the dominant tendency among many others hardly less powerful. Mr. Wilde's worship of beauty is proverbial—it has made a latter-day myth of him before his time; and yet, at least in these essays, his gift of comic perception is above it, and, rightly viewed, all his "flute-toned" periods are written in the service of the comic muse. When he is not of malice aforethought humorous, when he seems to be arguing with serious face enough, it is not simply that he may smile behind his mask at the astonishment, not to say terror, of a public he has from the first delighted in shocking. He loves to hear it call him "dangerous," as some men delight to be called "roué."

There will be many who will, as the phrase is, take him seriously; but let me assure them that Mr. Wilde is not of the number. It all depends what one means by the phrase; for I, for one, take Mr. Wilde very seriously as a creator of work which gives me much and various new pleasure: he is so absolutely alive at every point, so intensely practical—if people could only see it—and therefore so refreshingly unsentimental: he is wittier than is quite fair in a man of his nationality, and he often writes prose that one loves to say over for mere pleasure of ear—his own literary touchstone. The artistic temperament should delight in him; for the serious in the pursuit of literary pleasure he is as serious as every new joy must be. It is only in the domain of thought where it is rather funny to see him taken with such open mouth. Not that Mr. Wilde is not a thinker. and a very subtle one, too; but it is rather, so to say, as a damascener of thought, than a forger of it, that he is to be regarded.

.   .   .   .

It belongs to Mr. Wilde's paradoxical method that he should continually play on the convertibility of terms. Thus the whole contention of

his essays on criticism is that criticism and creation are essentially one and the same, or, at least,
that they necessarily dovetail one into the other;
and yet towards the end of this essay we find
Gilbert saying: "It is certain that the subject-
matter at the disposal of creation is always dimin-
ishing, while the subject-matter of criticism increases daily. Here we have two terms crystallised
once more to their hard-and-fast everyday meaning, while all through they have been used as
convertible. This is apt to bewilder. As a rule,
however, Mr. Wilde gains his effects by adhering
to the concrete signification of words. This re-
duces some of his contentions to a mere question of terms. One often feels: Now, if that
word were but changed for another, for which it
really stands, there would be nothing further to
say. But that, of course, would not do for Mr.
Wilde, nor indeed for us, to whom, presumably,
subject is nought and treatment is all. Occasionally, by this means, it follows that Mr. Wilde
seems to beg the question; as, for instance, in his
remarks on morality in art, when he says, "All
art is universal," he is using the word in its
narrow relative sense, he does not mean by it the
same as those who use it seriously against cer-

tain schools and forms of art: though they say "universal" they mean "unspiritual," and that is the meaning many people will attach to the word in Mr. Wilde's phrase. They will thus be quite unnecessarily shocked by a mere quibble of words, and their real position is left unassailed; the real question at issue being whether or not there is certain art which is dangerous to the spirit, of which we should feel as Mr. Pater says in "Marius": "This is what I may not look at." If life be really a struggle between higher and lower, if art is anything more than a form of sensuous indulgence, this is a question to be answered. Mr. Wilde does not leave us quite clear as to his side in the matter, though he seems to lay over-much stress on the sensuous side of art, a side which is after all external and impossible without an informing formative soul. He echoes, too, Gautier's tirades against "virtue" and Mr. Swinburne's

"What ailed us, O gods, to desert you
    For the creeds that refuse and restrain?"

and says hard things of chastity and self-sacrifice—really a very "young" and illogical position in an age which has accepted evolution. He quotes M. Renan to the effect that "Nature cares little about chastity"; but does that prove anything save that Nature is always behind the age, as Mr. Wilde tells us in another place? Surely it is by such ideals, of which, once seen, the beauty haunts him through all his sinnings, that man evolves at all, striving and failing and striving, till slowly what was once the ideal becomes the instinct.

But I am not recking my own rede, and am in danger of growing quite "heated," as they say of politicians, while Mr. Wilde is doubtless smiling in his sleeve.

Let us leave contention and enjoy. I have referred to two or three of the interesting qualities of these papers. They are so absolutely alive. Every sentence is full of brain. There is no padding, no vagueness; all is "thought out," as the painters say. One has that safe untroubled feeling in reading that Matthew Arnold's calm dissecting method gives us—though needless to say, the austerity of the "Essays in Criticism" is a very different thing from this luxuriously coloured prose: however difficult the thesis, we leave it to the writer with perfect confidence that he will

No. 16 Tite Street.
Page 192

speedily make all clear. Mr. Wilde has, indeed,
a rare power of keeping his eye steadily "on the
object." It is doubtless, too, a part of his per-
versity that while, as we have seen, he will, when
it suits him, adhere rigidly to the fixed signification
of words, he can at other times exercise a quite
remarkable power of reducing them to their elements, of remorselessly forcing them to say what
they really mean. . . .

Mr. Wilde's delight in words for their own sake
is quite Rabelaisian. He loves so to spread them
in heaps, like a child bathing its hands in rich,
many-coloured beads, that sometimes he is in
danger of a lack of proportion, and catalogues
that remind us of the Whitmanese. But some of
his tapestries in which, in a brief pageant, he
shows us again the Trojan War, or Dante thread-
ing the circles of his great dream, are beautiful;
and in passages such as the following his technical
knowledge of artistic methods, especially handi-
craft, give us a sense of surefootedness, a pre-
Raphaelite distinction of impression very quick-
ening to the imagination:

"The sculptor hewed from the marble block the
great white-limbed Hermes that slept within it.
The waxers and gilders of images gave the tone

and texture to the statue, and the world, when it saw it, worshipped and was dumb. He poured the glowing bronze into the mould of sand, and the river of red metal cooled into noble curves, and took the impress of the body of a god. With enamel or polished jewels he gave sight to the sightless eyes. The hyacinth-like curls grew crisp beneath his graver. . . . All subtle arts belonged to him also. He held the gem against the revolving disc, and the amethyst became the purple couch for Adonis, and across the veined sardonyx sped Artemis with her hounds. . . . The potter sat in his shed, and flower-like from the silent wheel the vase rose up beneath his hands."

This comes of an almost Renaissance gift of curiosity and a power of various appreciation, which is one of Mr. Wilde's surprises, as it is one of the most robust signs about his work. His reverence for Milton means much. In fact, since "The Decay of Lying," which is here reprinted, Mr. Wilde has become quite newly significant. One hardly knows yet what to expect of him, but we may be quite sure that these essays and "Dorian Gray" are but preludes. At present a delicate literary affectation, which is probably irritating to most, but rather a charm to those who know

what it means, a suggestion of insincerity, a refusal to commit himself, to be "the slave of his
own opinions," makes him somewhat of a riddle.
Will it seem too serious to remind Mr. Wilde of
one of his earliest sonnets—"Is That Time Dead?"
I think not.

Meanwhile, these "Intentions" are delightful
reading, especially, as was said, for their humour;
and if I have failed to do them justice, it is but a
proof of Mr. Wilde's paradox that it is impossible
to do justice to anything we care about.

CHAPTER VIII

THE PICTURE OF DORIAN GRAY.

Perhaps the book that created the most general discussion and criticism at this period was "The Picture of Dorian Gray," which appeared originally in *Lippincott's Magazine* in July, 1890, as the complete novel for that issue. Mr. J. M. Stoddart, then managing *Lippincott's Magazine,* had himself proposed to Wilde, while on a visit to London in the summer of 1889, that he should write a novel for *Lippincott's.* Wilde at first demurred on the ground that he had not tried his hand on a long and sustained story, but finally gave his consent. The story seems to have simmered in his mind for some time, though after he had once begun it, it was quickly completed. Wilde has himself said that he wrote it in a few days. In a preface to this story, written for a later edition in book form, Mr. Basil Ward, the artist, tells of the genesis of the story. It goes back to the year 1884, when Oscar Wilde was often in Mr. Ward's studio. One of Mr. Ward's sitters was a young man of such peculiar beauty that his friends had nicknamed him "The Radiant Youth." Each afternoon Wilde watched the work advance, enchanting everybody meanwhile with brilliant talk, until at last the portrait was finished and its original had gone his way—rejoicing, without doubt, to be at liberty.

"What a pity," sighed Wilde, "that such a glorious creature should ever grow old!"

"Yes, it is indeed," answered Mr. Ward. "How delightful it would be if 'Dorian' could remain exactly as he is while the portrait aged and withered in his stead. I wish it might be so!"

And that was all. "I occupied myself," says Mr. Ward, "with the picture for perhaps a quarter of an hour, during which Wilde smoked reflectively, but uttered not one word. He arose presently and sauntered to the door, merely nodding as he left the room.

"Family affairs called me by-and-by from London. I saw no more of either Wilde or 'Gray.'

"One day years afterward this book fell into my hands—I cannot remember where or how, although it startled me to find the germ, sown carelessly in idle talk, expanded by the writer's art into 'The Picture of Dorian Gray.' Wilde must have brooded long upon the theme. 'The Radiant Youth' was the very opposite of Wilde's bad hero; but such was the author's love of paradox that this antithesis of character was just the thing to fascinate his poet's mind."

Since its publication in *Lippincott's Magazine* twelve distinctive editions of "The Picture of Dorian Gray" have been printed in English. But two of these were authorized and sanctioned by the author, and in these two editions some alterations and additions have been made to the original text. A translation appeared in Paris in 1895, and was followed by two editions in cheaper form. Two translations, one by Johannes Gaulke, the other by Felix Paul Greve, appeared in Germany, and there are also translations in Italian and Swedish. When it first appeared the novel seems to have been better received by the critics in America than in England. Julian Hawthorne thus reviewed it shortly after its appearance in *Lippincott's*:

Mr. Oscar Wilde, the apostle of beauty, has in the July number of *Lippincott's Magazine* a novel, or romance (it partakes of the qualities of both), which everybody will want to read. It is a story strange in conception, strong in interest, and fitted with a tragic and ghastly climax. Like many stories of its class, it is open to more than one interpretation; and there are doubtless critics who will deny that it has any meaning at all. It is, at all events, a salutary departure from the ordinary English novel, with the hero and heroine of different social stations, the predatory black sheep, the curate, the settlements, and Society. Mr. Wilde, as we all know, is a gentleman of an original and audacious turn of mind, and the commonplace is scarcely possible to him. Besides, his advocacy of novel ideas in life, art, dress and demeanor had led us to expect surprising things from him; and in this literary age it is agreed that a man may best show the best there is in him by writing a book. Those who read Mr. Wilde's story in the hope of finding in it some compact and final statement of his theories of life and manners will be satisfied in some respects, and dissatisfied in others; but not many will deny that the book is a remarkable one and would attract attention even had it appeared without the author's name on the title-page.

"The Picture of Dorian Gray" begins to show

its quality in the opening pages. Mr. Wilde's writing has what is called "color"—the quality that forms the mainstay of many of Ouida's works —and it appears in the sensuous descriptions of nature and of the decorations and environment of the artistic life. The general aspect of the characters, and the tenor of their conversation, remind one a little of "Vivian Gray" and a little of "Pelham"; but the resemblance does not go far: Mr. Wilde's objects and philosophy are different from those of either Disraeli or Bulwer. Meanwhile, his talent for aphorisms and epigrams may fairly be compared with theirs: some of his clever sayings are more than clever—they show real insight and a comprehensive grasp. Their wit is generally cynical; but they are put into the mouth of one of the characters, Lord Harry, and Mr. Wilde himself refrains from definitely committing himself to them; though one cannot help suspecting that Mr. Wilde regards Lord Harry as being an uncommonly able fellow. Be that as it may, Lord Harry plays the part of the Old Harry in the story, and lives to witness the destruction of every other person in it. He may be taken as an imaginative type of all that is most evil and most refined in modern civilization—

a charming, gentle, witty, euphemistic Mephistopheles, who deprecates the vulgarity of goodness,
and muses aloud about "those renunciations that
men have unwisely called virtue, and those natural
rebellions that wise men still call sin." Upon
the whole, Lord Harry is the most ably portrayed
character in the book, though not the most original
in conception.   Dorian Gray himself is as nearly
a new idea in fiction as one has nowadays a right
to expect. If he had been adequately realized
and worked out, Mr. Wilde's first novel would
have been remembered after more meritorious ones
were forgotten.   But, even as "nemo repente fuit
turpissimus," so no one, or hardly any one, creates
a thoroughly original figure in fiction at a first
essay.   Dorian never quite solidifies.   In fact, his
portrait is rather the more real thing of the two.
But this needs explanation.

The story consists of a strong and marvellous
central idea, illustrated by three characters, all
men.   There are a few women in the background,
but they are only mentioned: they never appear
to speak for themselves.   There is, too, a valet
who brings in his master's breakfasts, and a chem-
ist who, by some scientific miracle, disposes of
a human body; but, substantially, the book is

taken up with the artist who paints the portrait, with his friend Lord Harry aforesaid, and with Dorian Gray, who might, so far as the story goes, stand alone. He and his portrait are one, and their union points the moral of the tale.

The situation is as follows: Dorian Gray is a youth of extraordinary physical beauty and grace, and pure and innocent of soul. An artist sees him and fall æsthetically in love with him, and finds in him a new inspiration in his art, both direct and general. In the lines of his form and features, and in his coloring and movement, are revealed fresh and profound laws; he paints him in all guises and combinations, and it is seen and admitted on all sides that he has never before painted so well. At length he concentrates all his knowledge and power in a final portrait, which has the vividness and grace of life itself, and, considering how much both of the sitter and of the painter is embodied in it, might almost be said to live. This portrait is declared by Lord Harry to be the greatest work of modern art; and the painter himself thinks so well of it that he resolves never to exhibit it, even as he would shrink from exposing to public gaze the privacies of his own nature.

On the day of the last sitting a singular incident occurs. Lord Harry, meeting on that occasion for the first time with Dorian, is no less
impressed than was Hallward, the artist, with the
youth's radiant beauty and freshness. But whereas Hallward would keep Dorian unspotted from
the world, and would have him resist evil temptations and the allurements of corruption, Lord
Harry, on the contrary, with a truly Satanic ingenuity, discourses to the young man on the matchless delights and privileges of youth. Youth is
the golden period of life: youth never comes again:
in youth only are the senses endowed with divine
potency; only then are joys exquisite and pleasures
unalloyed. Let it therefore be indulged without
stint. Let no harsh and cowardly restraints be
placed upon its glorious impulses. Men are virtuous through fear and selfishness. They are too
dull or too timid to take advantage of the godlike
gifts that are showered upon them in the morning
of existence; and before they can realize the folly
of their self-denial, the morning has passed, and
weary day is upon them, and the shadows of night
are near. But let Dorian, who is matchless in the
vigor and resources of his beauty, rise above the
base shrinking from life that calls itself goodness.

Let him accept and welcome every natural impulse of his nature. The tragedy of old age is not that one is old, but that one is young: let him so live that when old age comes he shall at least have the satisfaction of knowing that no opportunity of pleasure and indulgence has escaped untasted.

This seductive sermon profoundly affects the innocent Dorian, and he looks at life and at himself with new eyes. He realizes the value as well as the transitoriness of that youth and beauty which hitherto he had accepted as a matter of course and as a permanent possession. Gazing on his portrait, he laments that it possesses the immortality of loveliness and comeliness that is denied to him; and, in a sort of imaginative despair, he utters a wild prayer that to the portrait, and not to himself, may come the feebleness and hideousness of old age; that whatever sins he may commit, to whatever indulgences he may surrender himself, not upon him but upon the portrait may the penalties and disfigurements fall. Such is Dorian's prayer; and, though at first he suspects it not, his prayer is granted. From that hour, the evil of his life is registered upon the face and form of his pictured presentment, while he himself goes unscathed. Day by day, each fresh sin that he commits stamps its mark of degradation upon the painted image. Cruelty, sensuality, treachery, all nameless crimes, corrupt and render hideous the effigy on the canvas: he sees in it the gradual pollution and ruin of his soul, while his own fleshly features preserve unstained all the freshness and virginity of his sinless youth. The contrast at first alarms and horrifies him; but at length he becomes accustomed to it, and finds a sinister delight in watching the progress of the awful change. He locks up the portrait in a secret chamber, and constantly retires thither to ponder over the ghastly miracle. No one but he knows or suspects the incredible truth; and he guards like a murder-secret this visible revelation of the difference between what he is and what he seems. This is a powerful situation; and the reader may be left to discover for himself how Mr. Wilde works it out.

Miss Anne Hollingsworth Wharton, a critic of fine literary taste, also reviewed the novel at length as follows:

In all ages and climes mankind has found delight in romances based upon the mystic, the improbable, and the impossible, from the days when the Norse poets sang their Sagas through long Northern nights, and the fair Schéhérezade, under Southern moons, charmed her bloodthirsty lord by her tales of wonder, to our own day, when Stevenson and Crawford and Haggard hold fancy spell-bound by their entirely improbable stories. Scott and Bulwer played with master hands upon the love of the mysterious and supernatural inherent in mankind; Dickens and others have essayed to gratify its demands, but with less daring, and, having an eye always on the moorings of the actual, their success has been less marked. With the elder Hawthorne such romance-writing seemed the natural outgrowth of an exquisitely sensitive and spiritual nature, while among later French writers Théophile Gautier and Edmond About have entered into the domain of the impossible as into the natural heritage of their genius, sporting in its impalpable ether with the playful abandon of a fish in the sea or a bird in the air, hampered by no bond of the actual, weighted by no encumbrance of the material.

It is not strange that the great influx of realistic novels that have flowed in upon the last decade should be followed by a revulsion to the impossible in fiction. Men and women, wearied with meeting the same characters and events in so-called romance that they encounter in every-day life, or saddened by the depressing, if dramatic, pictures of Tolstoi and the cool vivisection of humanity presented by Ibsen, turn with a sense of rest and refreshment to the guidance of those who, like Robert Louis Stevenson and Rider Haggard, lead them suddenly into the mystic land of wonder, or, like Marion Crawford and Mrs. Oliphant, delight to draw them, by gentle and easy stages, from the midst of a well-appointed setting of every-day life into the shadowy border-land that lies between the real and the unreal. Much of the success of such romance-writing rests upon the rebound, natural to humanity, from intense realism to extreme ideality; more, perhaps, upon the fact that this age which is grossly material is also deeply spiritual. With these two facts well in view, Mr. Oscar Wilde has fallen into line, and entered the lists with some of the most successful masters of fiction. In his novel, "The Picture of Dorian Gray," written for the July *Lippincott's,* Mr. Wilde, like Balzac and the authors of "Faust" and "John Inglesant," presents to us the drama of a human soul, while like Gautier and About, he surrounds his utterly impossible story with a richness and depth of colouring and a grace and airiness of expression that make the perusal of its pages an artistic delight.

If Mr. Wilde's romance resembles the productions of some of the writers of the French school in its reality and tone, it still more strongly resembles Mr. Stevenson's most powerfully wrought fairy tale, "Dr. Jekyll and Mr. Hyde," although the moral of the story is brought out even more plainly—as plainly, indeed, as in the drama of "Faust." In both Mr. Stevensons's and Mr. Wilde's stories there is a transformation or substitution. In one the soul of Dr. Jekyll appears under different exteriors; in the other some fine influence passes from the soul of Dorian Gray into his portrait and there works a gradual and subtle change upon the pictured lineaments. Although Mr. Wilde's extravagance is far less dramatic than that of Mr. Stevenson, it has the advantages of richer colouring, and a more human setting, if we may so express it. The characters in "The Picture of Dorian Gray" enjoy life more than Mr. Stevenson's creations, who seem to have had so dull a time of it at the best that they might have been expected to welcome a tragedy, as a relief to the

tedium of their daily lives.   Mr. Utterson, we are
told, was good, but he was evidently not particularly happy, which was the case with the other personages of the drama, with the exception of those
who were signally wretched.   On the other hand,
Mr. Wilde's characters are happy during their
little day.   Their world is a luxurious, perfumed
land of delight, until sin transforms it, and, even
after Lord Henry has corrupted the nature of
Dorian Gray with evil books and worldly philosophy, he occasionally drinks of the waters of Lethe
and enjoys some fragments of what may be called
happiness, while Lord Henry himself seems to de-
rive a certain satisfaction from the practice of his
Mephistophelian art and in his entire freedom
from the restraints of conscience.   In a tale of
the impossible it is not required that the writer
should be true to life, animate or inanimate, yet
in the fact that there are glimpses of light through
the clouds that surround his *dramatis personæ,*
that they inhabit a world in which the laburnum
hangs out yellow clusters in June, and the clematis
robes itself with purple stars, and the sun sheds
gold and the moon silver, despite the tragedy that
touches the lives of its inhabitants, is not Mr.
Wilde quite as true to nature as to art?

The reader may reasonably question the author's good taste in displaying at such length his knowledge of antique decoration and old-world crime as in Chapter IX, which, besides being somewhat tiresome, clogs the dramatic movement of the story. Yet, on the other hand, it must be admitted that none but an artist and an apostle of the beautiful could have so systematically portrayed the glowing hues and perfumes of the garden in which Dorian Gray had first presented to his lips the cup of life, and none other could have so pictured the luxurious surroundings of his home, for whose embellishment the known world had been searched for hangings, ornaments, and bric-à-brac. Amid such an *entourage* of modern London life, with its sybaritic indulgence, its keenness of wit, and its subtle intelligence, Mr. Wilde places his characters and works out his miracle.

Viewing his own portrait, just completed by an artist friend, Dorian Gray turns from it filled with envy and dissatisfaction, because it has been whispered in his ear that youth is the supremest possession in life, and that when youth and beauty have fled from his face and form this pictured presentment will live forever, a perpetual mockery of himself, whom withering age has overtaken.

Under the influence of his evil genius, Lord Henry
Wotton, Dorian Gray utters a prayer that he may
always remain young, and the portrait alone reveal
the ravages of time, sin and sorrow.   The realiza-
tion of this idea is the theory of Mr. Wilde's
romance, and the air of probability with which he
has endowed the absolutely impossible evidences
the artistic and dramatic power of the writer.
The portrait of Dorian Gray, painted in days of
innocence and loveliness, when his mere presence
symbolized to the artist the entire harmony between beauty of body and beauty of soul, changes
day by day with the degradation of his nature,
while the living Dorian Gray, after years of sin,
remorseless cruelty, and corruption of thought and
action, preserves all the grace and fairness of his
Antinöus-like youth.

Love in this romance is an incident, not its
crowning event, although an important incident
as a revelation of the character of Dorian Gray.
The reader never meets Sibyl Vane; he merely sees
her on the stage and hears of her from the lips
of her lover; yet even thus she appeals to us as
an exquisite personation of maidenhood with all its
purity and all its tenderness.   As shadowy an outline as the fair child whom Bulwer allows to cap-

tivate the imagination of Kenelm Chillingly, who caught butterflies, talked philosophy, and died young, yet who in her brief transit across his path realized to his poetic soul all the best possibilities of life, spiritual and material, Sibyl Vane comes to us girt about with ideal charm, to fulfill her widely different mission, which was to reveal to Dorian Gray the sad fact that his soul had passed beyond her sweet and ennobling influence. His artistic and intellectual senses were touched by her beauty and dramatic power, but to the beauty that made her worthy to be loved his eyes were blind, his heart was insensible. The tragedy of the story, the climax of the situation, is not the death of Sibyl Vane, nor even the pitiless murder of the friend who dared to give Dorian Gray good counsel, but the disclosure that Dorian's soul, once open to all good influences, had, by yielding to the malign domination of his evil genius, passed beyond the reach of love, pity or remorse.

It is needless to say that Dorian Gray is not a very substantial character. The most entertaining, though not the most exemplary, personage of the story is Lord Henry Wotton, who by his preaching and practice of the doctrine of hedonism leads Dorian Gray into all known and unknown evil, until finally his darkling shadow outreaches in depravity the imagination of his tempter. When his victim has sunk so low in sin that the world shuns him, Lord Henry still enjoys his gay, conscienceless existence, and continues to utter the persiflage that constitutes much of the attraction of the book as well of his society. Debonair, witty, learned, giving expression to aphorisms as keen as the sayings of Thackeray's characters, with the moral element eliminated, and as cynical as those of Norris, with exquisite taste and the fascination of a finished man of the world, Lord Henry belongs as truly, on the material side of his nature, to the life of to-day, as he appertains on its spiritual side to the region of Pluto. A gay child of the great London social world, he hovers airily around and about the emotions of life, declaring that death is the only thing that ever terrifies him, and that death and vulgarity are the only facts in the nineteenth century that one cannot explain away. The climax of Lord Henry's sardonic worldliness is reached when he becomes the spectator of his own domesticity, if he may be said to have any, and speaks to Dorian of his divorce from his wife as one of the latest sensations of London, remarking *apropos* of his music: "The man with whom my wife ran away played Chopin exquisitely. Poor Victoria! I was very fond of her. The house is rather lonely without her."

Lord Henry is so entirely true to himself and the worst that is in him that towards the close of the book, when Dorian announces that he is "going to be good," and begs his friend not to poison another young life with the book with which he had corrupted his, we find ourselves trembling for Dorian's one remaining ally, especially when he exclaims: "My dear boy, you are really beginning to moralize. You will soon be going about warning people against all the sins of which you have grown tired. You are much too delightful to do that. Besides, it is no use. You and I are what we are, and we will be what we will be." Had not the hero stabbed himself, or his picture (which was it?), it is only a question of time how soon Dorian Gray, with the slightest obtrusion of conscience, would have ceased to charm him who had welcomed him as a *débutant* on the Stage of Pleasure, where, to use his favorite saying, "the only way to get rid of a temptation is to yield to it." Dorian Gray struggling against the temptations of the world would have proved an inartistic and disturbing element in the life of Lord Henry.

All that is needed to complete the tale is Lord Henry's own comment on the highly dramatic taking-off of his friend. This chapter Mr. Wilde, true to his artistic instinct, has not finished, preferring to leave appetite unappeased, rather than to create satiety by making his Mephistopheles say precisely what one would expect him to say under the circumstances.

The most notable review of "The Picture of Dorian Gray," written in England at the time of its publication, was one which appeared in *The Bookman* from the pen of Mr. Walter Pater. It is hardly satisfying because there is not a sufficient expression of opinion regarding the novel itself. Of Wilde himself, Mr. Pater says:

"There is always something of an excellent talker about the writings of Mr. Oscar Wilde; and in his hands, as happens so rarely with those who practise it, the form of dialogue is justified by its being really alive. His general laughter-loving sense of life and its enjoyable intercourse goes far to obviate any crudity that may be in the paradox, with which, as with the bright and shining truth which often underlies it, Mr. Wilde, startling his 'countrymen,' carries on, more perhaps than any other writer, the brilliant critical work of Matthew Arnold. 'The Decay of Lying,' for instance, is all but unique in its half humorous, yet wholly convinced, presentment of certain valuable truths of criticism. Conversational ease, the fluidity of life, felicitous expression are qualities which have a natural alliance to the successful writing of fiction; and side by side with Mr. Wilde's 'Intentions' (so he entitles his critical efforts) comes a novel, certainly original, and affording the reader a fair opportunity of comparing his practice as a creative artist with many a precept he has denounced as critic concerning it."

Of the book itself Mr. Pater later goes on to say: "A true Epicureanism aims at a complete though harmonious development of man's entire organism. To lose the moral sense therefore, for instance, the sense of sin and righteousness, as Mr. Wilde's hero—his heroes are bent on doing as speedily, as completely as they can—is to lose, or lower organism, to become less complex, to pass from a higher to a lower degree of development. . . . Dorian himself, though certainly a quite unsuccessful experiment in Epicureanism, in

life as a fine art, is (till his inward spoiling takes
visible effect suddenly, and in a moment, at the
end of his story) a beautiful creation. But his
story is also a vivid, though carefully considered
exposure of the corruption of a soul, with a very
plain moral, pushed home, to the effect that vice
and crime make people coarse and ugly. . . ."

A number of bitter attacks appeared, scoring
the book as immoral. This roused Wilde's indignation and he wrote several letters in reply to
these criticisms. The following letters published
in the *St. James Gazette* during this controversy
have a special interest as evincing Wilde's ideas
on art and ethics:

To THE EDITOR OF THE *St. James Gazette:*
Sir—I have read your criticism of my story,
"The Picture of Dorian Gray," and I need hardly
say that I do not propose to discuss its merits or
demerits, its personalities or its lack of personality.
England is a free country, and ordinary English
criticism is perfectly free and easy. Besides, I
must admit that, either from temperament, or
from taste, or from both, I am quite incapable of
understanding how any work of art can be criti-

cised from a moral standpoint. The sphere of art and the sphere of ethics are absolutely distinct and separate; and it is to the comparison between the two that we owe the appearance of Mrs. Grundy, that amusing old lady who represents the only original form of humour that the middle classes of this country have been able to produce. What I do object to most strongly is, that you should have placarded the town with posters on which was printed in large letters: Mr. Oscar Wilde's Latest Advertisement; A Bad Case.

Whether the expression "A Bad Case" refers to my book or to the present position of the Government, I cannot tell. What was silly and unnecessary was the use of the term "Advertisement."

I think I may say without vanity—though I do not wish to appear to run vanity down—that of all men in England, I am the one who requires least advertisement. I am tired to death of being advertised. I feel no thrill when I see my name in a paper. The chronicler does not interest me any more. I wrote this book entirely for my own pleasure and it gave me very great pleasure to write it. Whether it becomes popular or not is a matter of absolute indifference to me.

I am afraid, sir, that the real advertisement is your cleverly written article. The English public, as a mass, takes no interest in a work of art until it is told that the work in question is immoral, and your *réclame* will, I have no doubt, largely increase the sale of the magazine; in which sale, I may mention with some regret, I have no pecuniary interest. I remain, sir, your obedient servant,

OSCAR WILDE.

16 Tite Street, Chelsea, June 25.

June 26, 1890.

TO THE EDITOR OF THE *St. James Gazette:*

Sir—In your issue of to-day you state that my brief letter published in your columns is the "best reply" I can make to your article upon "Dorian Gray." This is not so. I do not propose to fully discuss the matter here, but I feel bound to say that your article contains the most unjustifiable attack that has been made upon any man of letters for many years. The writer of it, who is quite incapable of concealing his personal malice, and so in some measure destroys the effect he wishes to produce, seems not to have the slightest idea of the temper in which a work of art should be approached. To say that such a book as mine should be "chucked into the fire" is silly. That is what one does with newspapers.

Of the value of pseudo-ethical criticism in dealing with artistic work I have spoken already. But as your writer has ventured into the perilous grounds of literary criticism, I ask you to allow me, in fairness not only to myself but to all men to whom literature is a fine art, to say a few words about his critical method.

He begins by assailing me with much ridiculous virulence because the chief personages in my stories are "puppies." They *are* puppies. Does he think that literature went to the dogs when Thackeray wrote about puppydom? I think that puppies are extremely interesting from an artistic as well as from a psychological point of view. They seem to me to be certainly more interesting than prigs; and I am of opinion that Lord Henry Wotton is an excellent corrective of the tedious ideal shadowed forth in the semi-theological novels of our age.

He then makes vague and fearful insinuations about my grammar and my erudition. Now, as regards grammar, I hold that, in prose at any rate, correctness should always be subordinated to artistic effect and musical cadence; and any peculiarities of syntax that may occur in "Dorian Gray" are deliberately intended, and are introduced simply to show the value of the artistic theory in question. Your writer gives no instance of any such peculiarity. This I regret, because I do not think any such instances occur.

As regards erudition, it is always difficult, even for the most modest of us, to remember that other people do not know quite as much as one does oneself. I myself frankly admit I cannot imagine how a casual reference to Suetonius and Petronius Arbiter can be construed into evidence of a desire to impress an unoffending and ill-educated public by an assumption of superior knowledge. I should fancy that the most ordinary of scholars is perfectly well acquainted with the "Lives of the Cæsars" and with the "Satyricon." The "Lives of the Cæsars," at any rate, forms part of the ordinary curriculum at Oxford for those who take the Honour School of "Literæ Humaniores"; and as for the "Satyricon," it is popular even among passmen, though I suppose they are obliged to read it in translations.

The writer of the article then suggests that I, in common with that great and noble artist, Count

Tolstoi, take pleasure in a subject because it is dangerous. About such a suggestion there is this to be said. Romantic art deals with the exception and with the individual. Good people, belonging as they do to the normal, and so commonplace, type, are artistically uninteresting. But bad people are, from the point of view of art, fascinating studies. They represent colour, variety and strangeness. Good people exasperate one's reason; bad people stir one's imagination. Your critic, if I must give him so honourable a title, states that the people in my story have no counterpart in life; that they are, to use his vigorous if somewhat vulgar phrase, "mere catchpenny revelations of the non-existent." Quite so. If they existed they would not be worth writing about. The function of the artist is to invent, not to chronicle. There are no such people. If there were, I would not write about them. Life by its realism is always spoiling the subject-matter of art. The supreme pleasure in literature is to realize the non-existent.

And, finally, let me say this. You have reproduced, in a journalistic form, the comedy of "Much Ado About Nothing," and have, of course, spoiled it in your reproduction. The poor public, hearing from an authority as high as your own, that this is a wicked book that should be coerced and suppressed by a Tory Government, will, no doubt, rush to it and read it. But, alas! they will find that it is a story with a moral. And the moral is this: all excess, as well as all renunciation, brings its own punishment. The painter, Basil Hallward, worshipping physical beauty far too much, as most painters do, dies by the hand of one in whose soul he has created a monstrous and absurd vanity. Dorian Gray having led a life of mere sensation and pleasure, tries to kill Conscience and at that moment kills himself. Lord Henry Wotton seeks to be merely the spectator of life. He finds that those who reject the battle are more deeply wounded than those who take part in it. Yes: There is a terrible moral in "Dorian Gray"—a moral which the prurient will not be able to find in it, but which will be revealed to all whose minds are healthy. Is this an artistic error? I fear it is. It is the only error in the book.

I remain, sir, your obedient servant,

OSCAR WILDE.

To THE EDITOR OF THE *St. James Gazette:*
Sir—As you still keep up, though in a some-

what milder form than before, your attacks on me and my book, you not merely confer on me the right, but you impose upon me the duty to reply.

You state, in your issue of to-day, that I misrepresent you when I said that you suggested that a book so wicked as mine should be "suppressed and coerced by a Tory Government." Now you did not propose this, but you did suggest it. When you declare that you do not know whether or not the Government will take action about my book, and remark that the authors of books much less wicked have been proceeded against in law, the suggestion is quite obvious. In your complaint of misrepresentation you seem to me, sir, to have been not quite candid. However, as far as I am concerned the suggestion is of no importance. What is of importance is that the editor of a paper like yours should appear to countenance the monstrous theory that the Government of a country should exercise a censorship over imaginative literature. This is a theory against which I, and all men of letters of my acquaintance, protest most strongly; and any critic who admits the reasonableness of such a theory shows at once that he is quite incapable of understanding what literature is, and what are the rights that litera-

ture possesses. A Government might just as well
try to teach painters how to paint, or sculptors how
to model, as attempt to interfere with the style,
treatment and subject-matter of the literary artist;
and no writer, however eminent or obscure, should
ever give his sanction to a theory that would de-
grade literature far more than any didactic or so-
called immoral book could possibly do.

You then express your surprise that "so experienced a literary gentleman" as myself should imagine that your critic was animated by any feeling of personal malice towards him. The phrase
"literary gentleman" is a vile phrase; but let that
pass. I accept quite readily your assurance that
your critic was simply criticising a work of art
in the best way he could; but I feel that I was
fully justified in forming the opinion of him I
did. He opened his article by a gross personal
attack on myself. This, I need hardly say, was
an absolutely unpardonable error of critical taste.
There is no excuse for it, except personal malice;
and you, sir, should not have sanctioned it. A
critic should be taught to criticise a work of art
without making any reference to the personality
of the author. This, in fact, is the beginning of
criticism. However, it was not merely his per-

sonal attack on me that made me imagine that
he was actuated by malice. What really confirmed
me in my first impression was his reiterated as-
sertion that my book was tedious and dull. Now,
if I were criticising my book, which I have some
thoughts of doing, I think I would consider it
my duty to point out that it is far too crowded
with sensational incident and far too paradoxical
in style, as far, at any rate, as the dialogue goes.
I feel that from a standpoint of art these are the
two great defects in the book. But tedious and
dull the book is not. Your critic has cleared himself of the charge of personal malice, his denial
and yours being quite sufficient in the matter;
but he has only done so by a tacit admission that
he has really no critical instinct about literature
and literary work, which in one who writes about
literature, is, I need hardly say, a much graver
fault than malice of any kind.

Finally, sir, allow me to say this. Such an
article as you have published really makes one
despair of the possibility of any general culture
in England. Were I a French author, and my
book brought out in Paris, there is not a single
literary critic in France, on any paper of high
standing, who would think for a moment of criti-

cising it from an ethical standpoint. If he did so he would stultify himself, not merely in the eyes of all men of letters, but in the eyes of the majority of the public. You have yourself often spoken against Puritanism. Believe me, sir, Puritanism is never so offensive and destructive as when it deals with art matters. It is there that its influence is radically wrong. It is this Puritanism, to which your critic has given expression, that is always marring the artistic instinct of the English. So far from encouraging it, you should set yourself against it, and should try to teach your critics to recognise the essential difference between art and life. The gentleman who criticised my book is in a perfectly hopeless confusion about it, and your attempt to help him out by proposing that the subject-matter of art should be limited does not help matters. It is proper that limitations should be placed on actions. It is not proper that limitations should be placed on art. To art belong all things that are, and all things that are not, and even the editor of a London paper has no right to restrain the freedom of art in the selection of subject-matter.

I now trust, sir, that these attacks on me and on my book will cease. There are forms of advertisement that are unwarranted and unwarrantable. I am, sir, your obedient servant,

OSCAR WILDE.

16 Tite St., S. W., June 27.

TO THE EDITOR OF THE *St. James Gazette:*

Sir—In your issue of this evening you publish a letter from "A London Editor," which clearly insinuates in the last paragraph that I have in some way sanctioned the circulation of an expression of opinion, on the part of the proprietors of *Lippincott's Magazine,* of the literary and artistic value of my story of "The Picture of Dorian Gray."

Allow me, sir, to state that there are no grounds for this insinuation. I was not aware that any such document was being circulated; and I have written to the agents, Messrs. Ward & Lock—who cannot, I feel sure, be primarily responsible for its appearance—to ask them to withdraw it at once. No publisher should ever express an opinion on the value of what he publishes. That is a matter entirely for the literary critic to decide. I must admit, as one to whom contemporary literature is constantly submitted for criticism, that the only thing that ever prejudices me against a book is the lack of literary style; but I can quite understand how any ordinary critic would be strongly prejudiced against a work that was accompanied by a premature and unnecessary panegyric from the publisher. A publisher is simply a useful middleman. It is not for him to anticipate the verdict of criticism.

I may, however, while expressing my thanks to the "London Editor" for drawing my attention to this, I trust, purely American method of procedure, venture to differ from him in one of his criticisms. He states that he regards the expression "complete," as applied to a story, as a specimen of the "adjectival exuberance of the puffer!" Here, it seems to me, he sadly exaggerates. What my story is, is an interesting problem. What my story is not, is a "novelette"—a term which you have more than once applied to it. There is no such word in the English language as novelette. It should never be used. It is merely part of the slang of Fleet Street.

In another part of your paper, sir, you state that I received your assurance of the lack of malice in your critic "somewhat grudgingly." This is not so. I frankly said that I accepted that assurance "quite readily," and that your own denial and that of your critic were "sufficient." Nothing more generous could have been said. What I did feel was that you saved your critic from the charge of malice by convicting him of the unpardonable crime of lack of literary instinct. I still feel that. To call my book an ineffective attempt at allegory that, in the hands of Mr. Anstey, might have been made striking, is absurd. Mr. Anstey's sphere in literature, and my sphere are different—very widely different.

You then gravely ask me what rights I imagine literature possesses. That is really an extraordinary question for the editor of a newspaper such as yours to ask. The rights of literature, sir, are the rights of intellect.

I remember once hearing M. Renan say that he would sooner live under a military despotism than under the despotism of the church, because the former merely limited the freedom of the body, while the latter limited the freedom of mind. You say that a work of art is a form of action. It is not. It is the highest mode of thought.

In conclusion, sir, let me ask you not to force on me this continued correspondence by daily attacks. It is a trouble and a nuisance. As you assailed me first, I have a right to the last word.

Let that last word be the present letter, and leave my book, I beg you, to the immortality it deserves. I am, sir, your obedient servant,

OSCAR WILDE.

16 Tite St., S. W., June 28.

Still another book of Wilde's, a collection of short stories, "Lord Arthur Savile's Crime and Other Stories," appeared in July, 1891. This book was well received even by its reviewers. *The Athenæum* said: "Mr. Oscar Wilde's little book of stories is capital. They are delightfully humorous, witty and fresh, sparkling with good things, full of vivacity, and well put together."

For the writing of short stories Oscar Wilde had a peculiar facility. They appeared to cause him almost no labor, and he invented plots with the greatest ease. A friend of his relates that one morning to help out his brother, Willy Wilde, Oscar invented no less than six plots in less than a half hour. Willy Wilde afterwards wrote out the stories, and they proved very popular.

At this period André Gide met Wilde for the first time in Paris at a small dinner party, and says of his wonderful knack for story-telling: "We were a party of four, but three of us were content to listen. Wilde did not converse—he told tales. During the whole meal he hardly stopped." And these tales were drawn from no other source than Wilde's own brilliant fancy. He had a genius for improvisation."

This period indeed was a golden one in the life of Wilde—golden in the sense of prosperity and of personal triumph. "It was," to quote Gide again, "in 1891 that I met him for the first time. Wilde had then what Thackeray calls 'one of the greatest of a great man's qualities'—success. His manner and appearance were triumphant. His success was so assured that it seemed to go in front of him, and he had only to advance. His books were causing wonder and delight. All London was soon to rush to see his plays."

CHAPTER IX.

PLAYS AND PROSPERITY

"All London was soon to rush to see his plays." This indeed came to pass, and more than this has come to pass, for the plays of Oscar Wilde have found audiences in many countries—in America, in France, in Austria, in Germany, in Italy. "His plays," says the *Encyclopædia Brittanica,*" were perhaps the most original contribution to English dramatic writing during the period."

"Lady Windermere's Fan," which was produced at the St. James Theatre on February 20, 1892, was an immediate success, and has enjoyed a wide popularity since. It is full of the sparkling dialogue and brilliant epigrams that characterized other plays that followed in quick succession.

" 'Lady Windermere's Fan,' " said *The Spectator,* "as a specimen of true comedy is a head and shoulders above any of its contemporaries for some years syne. . . . It is a distinguishing note of Mr. Wilde that he has condescended to leave his business, and has written a workmanlike play as well as a good comedy. . . . A unique specimen in our day—as far as we know—absolutely unique —of the comedy of fine life and manners."

A correspondent of the Boston *Transcript* in the course of a long letter to his paper dealing with the evolution of Wilde from an æsthetic poet to a dramatist, says: "As a dramatic author, Mr. Wilde comes out of the bandbox like a new hat. He is so bright, new and altered in shape that you do not recognize the same old hat."

Later he goes on to speak of Wilde in his own home: "The Chippendale chairs in Mr. Wilde's house in Chelsea are all painted cream-white and are covered in white plush to match. One room is white and gold, another a harmony in yellows, and another a harmony in blues. The effect is by no means bad, though in so smoky a town as London a few finger-marks on the white chairs are not to be avoided. But finger-marks if they are long and lean enough are not unartistic or unbeautiful. Mr. Wilde's sanctum is a veritable chaos of book piles, slippers, pipes, cigarettes and manuscripts. Like most writers, he has made war on the dust-pan and brush, so that his servants have to watch for their chance when he is at the club or at tea with a party of 'souls.' Mr. Wilde is one of the original 'souls.' There are a few traits in the character of Mr. Wilde that make him unconventional if not unique. Conventionality is the one thing besides prolixity that smothers Oscar Wilde, so at any cost—even of common sense—he shuns both. A few months ago the writer remarked to Mr. Wilde that he did like a certain American writer of plays because of his affectation. 'Don't you really like him? I do,' said Wilde. 'I love affectation, it's charming!' A few weeks ago some one said to Mr. Wilde, 'That, Wilde, would not be lawful.' 'Oh, how delightfully interesting!' replied Wilde. 'I hate law and detest order; it's so dreadfully prosaic. Don't you loathe it, my dear boy?'

"Mr. Wilde's action before the curtain on the first night of 'Lady Windermere's Fan,' when he made a speech, whiffing a cigarette the while into the very face of the audience, was just the thing he loves to do, because it shocked the nerves of old-fashioned politeness and was, therefore, 'most unconventional.' "

A burlesque of "Lady Windermere's Fan," or rather of the eccentricities of its author, written by Mr. Charles Brookfield, had a run of several months at the Comedy Theatre, where it was put on, May, 1892. Charles Hawtrey took the leading rôle. The skit was entitled "The Poet and the Puppets." It derived its title evidently from a letter from Wilde published in *The Daily Telegraph* on the day that "Lady Windermere's Fan" began its run, and which was printed under the caption, "Puppets and Actors." This letter, giving Wilde's views of the actor's art, gave rise to much discussion and criticism. It ran as follows:

To THE EDITOR OF *The Daily Telegraph:*

Sir—I have just been sent an article that seems to have appeared in your paper some days ago, in which it is stated that, in the course of some remarks addressed to the Playgoers' Club on the occasion of my taking the chair at their last meeting, I laid down as an axiom that the stage is only "a frame furnished with a set of puppets."

Now it is quite true that I hold that the stage is to a play no more than a picture frame is to a painting; and that the actable value of a play has nothing whatsoever to do with its value as a work of art. In this century in England, to take an obvious example, we have had only two great plays—one is Shelley's "Cenci"; the other, Mr. Swinburne's "Atalanta in Calydon" —and neither of them is in any sense of the word an actable play. Indeed, the mere suggestion that stage presentation is any test of a work of art is quite ridiculous. In the production of Browning's plays, for instance, in London and at Oxford, what was being tested was obviously the capacity of the modern stage to represent, in any adequate measure or degree, works of introspective method and strange or sterile psychology. But the artistic value of "Strafford" or "In a Balcony" was settled when Robert Browning wrote their last lines. It is not, sir, by the mimes that the Muses are to be judged. So far, the writer of the article in question is right. Where he goes wrong is in saying that I described this frame—the stage—as being furnished "with a set of puppets." He admits that he speaks only by report; but he should have remembered, sir, that report is not merely a lying jade, which I personally could readily forgive her, but a jade who lies without lovely inventions —a thing that I, at any rate, can forgive her never.

What I really said was that the frame we call

the stage was "peopled with either living actors or moving puppets," and I pointed out briefly, of necessity, that the personality of the actor is often a source of danger in the perfect presentation of a work of art. It may distort. It may lead astray. It may be a discord in the tone of symphony. For anybody can act. Most people in England do nothing else. To be conventional is to be a comedian. To act a particular part, however, is a very different thing and a very difficult thing as well. The actor's aim is, or should be, to convert his own accidental personality into the real and essential personality of the character he is called upon to impersonate, whatever that character may be; or perhaps I should say that there are two schools of actors—the school of those who attain their effect by exaggeration of personality, and the school of those who attain it by suppression. It would take too long to discuss these schools, or to decide which of them the dramatist loves best. Let me note the danger of personality, and pass on to my puppets. There are many advantages in puppets. They never argue. They have no crude views about art. They have no private lives. We are never bothered by accounts of their virtues, or bored by recitals of their vices;

and when they are out of an engagement they never do good in public or save people from drowning! Nor do they speak more than is set down for them! They recognise the presiding intellect of the dramatist and have never been known to ask for their parts to be written up. They are admirably docile, and have no personalities at all. I saw lately, in Paris, a performance by certain puppets of Shakespeare's "Tempest" in M. Maurice Boucher's translation. Miranda was the image of Miranda because an artist had so fashioned her; and Ariel was true Ariel, because so had she been made. Their gestures were quite sufficient, and the words that seemed to come from their little lips were spoken by poets who had beautiful voices. It was a delightful performance, and I remember it still with delight, though Miranda took no notice of the flowers I sent her after the curtain fell. For modern plays, however, perhaps we had better have living players, for in modern plays actuality is everything. The charm —the ineffable charm of the unreal is here denied us, and rightly.

Suffer me one more correction. Your writer describes the author of the brilliant fantastic lecture on "The Modern Actor" as "a protégé" of mine. Allow me to state that my acquaintance with Mr. John Gray is, I regret to say, extremely recent, and that I sought it because he had already a perfected mode of expression both in prose and verse. All artists in this vulgar age need protection certainly. Perhaps they have always needed it. But the nineteenth century artist finds it not in Prince, or Pope, or patron, but in high indifference of temper; in the pleasure of the creation of beautiful things and the long contemplation of them; in disdain of what in life is common and ignoble; and in such felicitous sense of humour as enables one to see how vain and foolish is all popular opinion, and popular judgment, upon the wonderful things of art. These qualities Mr. John Gray possesses in a marked degree. He needs no other protection, nor indeed would he accept it.

I remain, sir, your obedient servant,

OSCAR WILDE.

London, Feb. 19th.

It was at the time of his success with "Lady Windermere's Fan" that Wilde wrote his famous play, "Salomé," the play that brought him the widest fame and which was the subject of such strange vicissitudes. It was written in French and was accepted by Sarah Bernhardt, who intended to produce it in London in June of 1892. But after it had been rehearsed, the Lord Chamberlain's Licenser of Plays refused to allow its performance on the ground that it was inadvisable to dramatize religious episodes. Oscar Wilde's indignation at this was so great that he thought seriously of leaving England and becoming a citizen of France. In an interview published in the *Pall Mall Gazette* on June 29, 1892, he said:

"Every rehearsal has been a source of intense pleasure to me. To hear my own words spoken by the most beautiful voice in the world has been the greatest artistic joy that it is possible to experience. So that you see, as far as I am concerned, I care very little about the refusal of the Lord Chamberlain to allow my play to be produced. What I do care about is this—that the Censorship apparently regards the stage as the lowest of all the arts, and looks on acting as a vulgar thing. The painter is allowed to take his subjects where he chooses. He can go to the great Hebrew, and Hebrew-Greek literature of the Bible and can paint Salomé dancing, or Christ on the Cross, or the Virgin with her Child. Nobody in-

terferes with the painter. Nobody says, 'Painting is such a vulgar art that you must not paint
sacred things.' The sculptor is equally free. He
can carve St. John the Baptist in his camel hair,
and fashion the Madonna or Christ in bronze or
in marble as he wills. Yet nobody says to him,
'Sculpture is such a vulgar art that you must not
carve sacred things.' And the writer, the poet—
he also is quite free. I can write about any subject I choose. For me there is no Censorship. I
can take any incident I like out of sacred literature and treat it as I choose and there is no one
to say to the poet, 'Poetry is such a vulgar art that
you must not use it in treating sacred subjects.'
But there is a Censorship over the stage and acting, and the basis of that Censorship is that, while
vulgar subjects may be put on the stage and acted,
while everything that is mean and low and shame-
ful in life can be portrayed by actors, no actor is to
be permitted to present under artistic conditions,
the great and ennobling subjects taken from the
Bible. The insult in the suppression of 'Salomé'
is an insult to the stage as a form of art and not
to me."

"I understand," said the interviewer, "that
Madame Bernhardt's engagements will not allow

her to play 'Salomé' at an invitation performance. We shall not see your play in London, then?"

"I shall publish 'Salomé.' No one has the right to interfere with me, and no one shall interfere with me. The people who are injured are the actors; the art that is vilified is the art of acting. I hold that this is as fine as any other art and to refuse it the right to treat great and noble subjects is an insult to the stage. The action of the Censorship in England is odious and ridiculous. What can be said of a body that forbids Massenet's 'Hérodiade,' Gounod's 'La Reine de Saba,' Rubinstein's 'Judas Maccabæus,' and allows 'Divorçons' to be placed on any stage? The artistic treatment of moral and elevating subjects is discouraged, while a free course is given to the representation of disgusting and revolting subjects."

"How came you to write 'Salomé' in French?"

"My idea of writing the play was simply this: I have one instrument that I know that I can command, and that is the English language. There was another instrument to which I had listened all my life, and I wanted once to touch this new instrument to see whether I could make any beautiful thing out of it. The play was written in Paris some six months ago, where I read it to some young poets, who admired it immensely. Of course there are modes of expression that a Frenchman of letters would not have used, but they give a certain relief or colour to the play. A great deal of the curious effect that Maeterlinck produces comes from the fact that he, a Flamand by grace, writes in an alien language. The same thing is true of Rossetti, who, though he wrote in English, was essentially Latin in temperament. A few weeks ago I met Madame Sarah Bernhardt at Sir Henry Irving's. She had heard of my play and asked me to read it to her. I did so, and she at once expressed a wish to play the title-rôle. Of course it has been a great disappointment to her and to her company not to have played this piece in London. We have been rehearsing for three weeks. The costumes, scenery and everything has been prepared, and we are naturally disappointed; still all are looking forward now to producing it for the first time in Paris, where the actor is appreciated and the stage is regarded as an artistic medium. It is remarkable how little art there is in the work of dramatic critics in England. You find column after column of description, but the critics rarely know how to praise an artistic work. The fact is, it requires an artist to praise art; anyone can pick it to pieces. For my own part, I don't know which I despise most, blame or praise. The latter, I think, for it generally happens that the qualities praised are those one regards with the least satisfaction oneself."

Hot with indignation, Wilde wrote as follows to a member of the *Gaulois* staff in Paris:

Sir—My resolution is deliberately taken. Since it is impossible to have a work of art performed in England, I shall transfer myself to another fatherland, of which I have long ago been enamoured. There is but one Paris, *voyez-vouz,* and Paris is France.

It is the abode of artists; nay, it is *la ville artiste*. I adore Paris. I also adore your language. To me there are only two languages in the world, French and Greek Here [in London] people are essentially anti-artistic and narrow-minded. Now the ostracism of "Salomé" will give you a fair notion of what people here consider venal and indecorous.

To put on the stage any person or persons connected with the Bible is impossible. On these grounds the Censorship has prohibited Saint-Saëns' "Samson et Dalila" and Massenet's "Hérodiade." Racine's superb tragedy of "Athalie" cannot be performed on an English stage. Really, one hardly knows whether the measure is the more hateful or ridiculous.

Of course, I do not deny that Englishmen possess certain practical qualities, but, as I am an artist, these qualities are not those which I can admire. Moreover, I am not at present an Englishman. I am an Irishman, which is by no means the same thing.

No doubt, I have English friends, to whom I am deeply attached, but as to the English, I do not love them. There is a great deal of hypocrisy in England, which you in France very justly find fault with.

The typical Briton is Tartuffe, seated in his shop behind the counter. There are numerous exceptions, but they only prove the rule.

OSCAR WILDE.

Madame Bernhardt promised to produce "Salomé" in her own theatre in Paris, but she did not fulfill her promise. Later, in his days of disgrace, Wilde tried to renew negotiations and to sell Madame Bernhardt the play outright, but the negotiations came to naught. The play was not produced until 1896, when it was brought out by Luigue Pöe in Paris. It was translated into German, when it created a furore after its production in Berlin in September, 1903. It was also brought out on the Italian stage. Its production both in London and New York in 1905-6 met with much adverse criticism, as did also Strauss's opera, whose libretto is translated from Wilde's play.

"Salomé" was published in book form in London early in 1893. It was severely attacked, but Henry Norman wrote a sympathetic review in *The Illustrated London News"*:

" . . . We can only say that so far from sacred things being scoffed at, the figure of John the Baptist, as he emerges from his dungeon to denounce the iniquities of the Tetrarch and his wife, or to tell the approaching doom of the former, is a singularly striking and noble one. Of course, Herod was a man of vile character. Herodias was a woman of abandoned tastes, Salomé was what no doubt the daughter of her mother in those days and those surroundings could not help being. But it is surely no disadvantage to the student of the first surroundings of Christianity to be helped by a dramatic mind to see these people as they were in reality.

"Mr. Wilde has taken the liberties with history which are more or less permitted to the poet and the dramatist. He represents Salomé as demanding the head of John, not in consequence of the promptings of her mother, but out of revenge for the refusal of the prophet to make any response to the infatuation which she had experienced for him at the sight of his white, thin body and pale, holy face—no doubt in such striking contrast to the other men whom she was accustomed to see. 'Jokanaan,' the Hebrew name for John, which Mr. Wilde uses, had repulsed her kisses while he lived, so she takes advantage of Herod's rash oath to force her kisses upon him dead. And Herod having with the utmost reluctance kept his word, is seized with such loathing afterward, that he orders Salomé to be killed, and the soldiers crush her beneath their shields. The dungeon is also an old well or cistern on the terrace outside the banqueting hall of Herod's palace, whereas we have every reason to believe that John was confined in a fortress at some distance from the capital of Judæa, Tiberias, where Herod undoubtedly held his court. These, however, are but minor points, the chief one being that Mr. Wilde has written a thrilling little tragedy, giving us a vivid picture of a fragment of that history in which we are all so deeply interested, tracing how the deed of blood which cut off the first Christian martyr may have grown up and developed in the minds of the perpetrators, painting in a few master-touches a splendid figure of the forerunner of Christ, and—in the eyes of many people the most important matter of all—presenting us with that peculiar pleasure which comes alone from the contemplation of a work of art duly conceived and skilfully executed."

For three years Wilde enjoyed a period of great prosperity, his plays were rapidly making him rich, for during this period he produced three other plays with great success. "A Woman of No Importance" began a successful run on April 19, 1893, and on January 3, 1895, "An Ideal Husband" was produced at the Haymarket, to be quickly followed by "The Importance of Being Earnest," which made its appearance at the St.

James Theatre on February 14 of the same year. These plays all proved highly popular in America as well, and indeed, at intervals have continued to delight the English-speaking audiences of two worlds. And the plays succeeded despite the fact that the critics in general were against them. Wilde seized the occasion of getting back at the critics in an interview published in the London *Sketch:*

"The critics subordinate the psychological interest of a play to its mere technique. As soon as a dramatist invents an ingenious situation, they compare him with Sardou, but Sardou is an artist not because of his marvellous instinct of stagecraft, but in spite of it."

To a question from the interviewer, suggesting that something more than literature was wanted in a play, Wilde replied:

"That is merely because the critics have always propounded the degrading dogma that the duty of the dramatist is to please the public. Rossetti did not weave words into sonnets to please the public, and Corot did not paint silver and grey twilights to please the public. The mere fact of telling an artist to adopt any particular form of art in order to please the public, makes him shun it. We shall never have a real drama in England until it is recognised that a play is as personal and individual a form of self-expression as a poem or a picture."

One voice, however, and that of a fellow-dramatist and a fellow-Irishman, proclaimed the triumph of Oscar Wilde as a playwright. George Bernard Shaw, early in 1895, said in *The Saturday Review:*

" . . . He has the property of making his critics dull. They laugh angrily at his epigrams, like a child who is coaxed into being amused in the very act of setting up a yell of rage and agony. They protest that the trick is obvious, and that such epigrams can be turned out by the score by any one light-minded enough to condescend to such frivolity. As far as I can ascertain, I am the only person in London who cannot sit down and write an Oscar Wilde play at will. The fact that his plays, though apparently lucrative, remain unique under these circumstances, says much for the self-denial of our scribes. In a certain sense Mr. Wilde is to me our only thorough playwright. He plays with everything: with wit, with philosophy, with drama, with actors and audience, with the whole theatre. Such a feat scandalises the Englishman, who can no more play with wit and philosophy than he can with a football or cricket-bat. He works at both, and has the consolation, if he cannot make people laugh, of being the best cricketer and footballer in the world. Now it is the mark of the artist that he will not work. Just as people with social ambitions will practise the meanest economies in order to live expensively, so the artist will starve his way through incredible toil and discouragement sooner than go and earn a week's honest wages. Mr. Wilde, an arch-artist, is so colossally lazy that he trifles even with the work by which an artist escapes work. He distils the very quintessence, and gets as product plays which are so unapproachably playful that they are the delight of every play-goer with twopenn'orth of brains. The English critic, always protesting that the drama should not be didactic, and yet always complaining if the dramatist does not find sermons in stones and good in everything, will be conscious of a subtle and pervading levity in 'An Ideal Husband.' All the literary dignity of the play, all the imperturb-able good sense and good manners with which Mr. Wilde makes his wit pleasant to his comparatively stupid audience, cannot quite overcome the fact that Ireland is of all countries the most foreign to England, and that to the Irishman (and Mr. Wilde is almost as actually Irish an Irishman as the Iron Duke of Wellington) there is nothing in the world quite so exquisitely comic as an Eng-lishman's seriousness. It becomes tragic, perhaps, when the Englishman acts on it; but that occurs too seldom to be taken into account, a fact which intensifies the humour of the situation, the total result being the Englishman utterly unconscious of his real self, Mr. Wilde keenly observant of it and playing on the self-unconsciousness with irre-sistible humour, and finally, of course, the Eng-lishman annoyed with himself for being amused at his own expense, and for being unable to con-vict Mr. Wilde of what seems an obvious mis-understanding of human nature. He is shocked, too, at the danger to the foundations of society when seriousness is publicly laughed at. And to complete the oddity of the situation, Mr. Wilde, touching what he himself reverences, is absolutely the most sentimental dramatist of the day."

At the height of his prosperity, when his plays were producing him a royal income, came the sudden fall of Oscar Wilde, like a bolt out of the blue. It is needless to dwell here upon his trial and disgrace: the facts are well known, or can easily be ascertained. On Saturday, May 25, 1895, he was sentenced to two years' imprisonment with hard labor, a part of which sentence he served in Wandsworth Prison and the balance in Reading Gaol.

Over Wilde's life and terrible sufferings during these two years it is best to draw a merciful curtain. Let the reader turn to "De Profundis" to know the intensity of that suffering and the bitterness of remorse. The book was made up from a series of letters written by Wilde during his prison period to his friend, Robert Ross.

"De Profundis," says Mr. William Archer in a review, "is a document the significance of which cannot be distilled in a single article. It is not the wonder of a week nor even the topic of a season. Psychologists will study it centuries hence, and so, I have little doubt, will lovers of literature. . . . An adequate criticism of the book would be nothing less than an exhaustive treatise on ethics, æsthetics, sociology, theology, psychology. It would

be a soul-searching, and an anatomy of the body politic."

In prison Wilde experienced the hard and bitter discipline of sorrow; he emerged from prison a changed and broken man. The following chapter describing a visit to Oscar Wilde just after his release, and his subsequent life in Paris, is taken from "Oscar Wilde: A Study," by André Gide, as translated by Mr. Stuart Mason. It is perhaps the best account that has been written of Wilde's latter days.

CHAPTER X.

FROM THE FRENCH OF ANDRÉ GIDE.

As soon as he came out of prison, Oscar Wilde went back to France. At Berneval, a quiet little village near Dieppe, a certain "Sebastian Melmoth" took up his abode. It was he. As I had been the last of his French friends to see him, I wanted to be the first to greet him on his return to liberty, and as soon as I could find out his address I hastened to him.

I arrived about midday without having previously announced my proposed visit. M. Melmoth, whom T—— with warm cordiality invited to Dieppe fairly frequently, was not expected back till the evening. He did not return till midnight.

It was as cold as winter. The weather was atrocious. The whole day I wandered about the deserted beach in low spirits and bored to death. How could Wilde have chosen Berneval to live in,

I wondered. It was positively mournful. Night came, and I went back to the hotel to engage a room, the same hotel where Melmoth was living —indeed, it was the only one in the place. The hotel, which was clean and pleasantly situated, catered only for second-class boarders, inoffensive folk enough, with whom I had to dine. Rather poor company for Melmoth, I thought.

Fortunately I had a book to read, but it was a gloomy evening, and at eleven o'clock I was just going to abandon my intention of waiting up for him when I heard the rumbling of carriage wheels. M. Melmoth had arrived, benumbed with cold. He had lost his overcoat on the way. And, now that he came to think of it, he remembered that a peacock's feather which his servant had brought him the previous evening was a bad omen, and had clearly foretold some misfortune about to befall him; luckily it was no worse. But as he was shivering with cold, the hotel was set busy to warm some whiskey for him. He hardly said "How do you do?" to me. In the presence of others, at least, he did not wish to appear to be at all moved. And my own emotion was almost immediately stilled on finding Sebastian Melmoth so plainly like the Oscar Wilde of old—no longer the frenzied poet of

Algeria, but the sweet Wilde of the days before the crisis; and I found myself taken back not two years, but four or five. There was the same dreamy look, the same amused smile, the same voice.

He occupied two rooms, the best in the hotel, and he had arranged them with great taste. Several books lay on the table, and among them he showed me my own "Nourritures Terrestres," which had been published lately. A pretty Gothic Virgin stood on a high pedestal in a dark corner.

Presently we sat down near the lamp, Wilde drinking his grog in little sips. I noticed, now that the light was better, that the skin of his face had become red and common-looking, and his hands even more so, though they still bore the same rings—one to which he was especially attached had in a reversible bezel an Egyptian scarabæus in lapis lazuli. His teeth were dreadfully decayed.

We began chatting, and I reminded him of our last meeting in Algiers, and asked him if he remembered that I had almost foretold the approaching catastrophe.

"Did you not know," I said, "almost for certain what was awaiting you in England? You saw the danger and rushed headlong into it, did you not?"

Here I think I cannot do better than copy out the pages on which I wrote shortly afterwards as much as I could remember of what he said.

"Oh, naturally," he replied, "of course I knew that there would be a catastrophe, either that or something else; I was expecting it. There was but one end possible. Just imagine—to go any further was impossible, and that state of things could not last. That is why there had to be some end to it, you see. Prison has completely changed me. I was relying on it for that. —— is terrible. He cannot understand that—he cannot understand that I am not taking up the same existence again. He accuses the others of having changed me—but one must never take up the same existence again. My life is like a work of art. An artist never begins the same work twice, or else it shows that he has not succeeded. My life before prison was as successful as possible. Now all that is finished and done with."

He lighted a cigarette and went on: "The public is so dreadful that it knows a man only by the last thing he has done. If I were to go back to Paris now, people would see in me only the convict. I do not want to show myself again before I have written a play. Till then I must be left

alone and undisturbed." And he added abruptly:
"Did I not do well to come here? My friends
wanted me to go to the South to recruit, because
at first I was quite worn out. But I asked them
to find me, in the North of France, a very small
place at the seaside, where I should see no one,
where it was very cold and there was hardly ever
any sun. Did I not do well to come and live at
Berneval? [Outside the weather was frightful.]
Here every one is most good to me—the Curé especially. I am so fond of the little church, and,
would you believe it, it is called *Notre Dame de
Liesse!* Now, is not that charming? And now
I know that I can never leave Berneval, because
only this morning the Curé offered me a perpetual
seat in the choir-stalls.

And the Custom-house men, poor fellows, are so
bored here with nothing to do, that I asked them if
they had not anything to read, and now I am giving them all the elder Dumas' novels. So I must
stay here, you see. And the children, oh, the children, they adore me. On the day of the Queen's
Jubilee I gave a grand fête and a big dinner, when
I had forty children from the school, all of them,
and the schoolmaster, to celebrate it. Is not that
absolutely charming? You know that I admire

the Queen very much.   I always have her portrait
with me."

And he showed me her portrait by Nicholson,
pinned on the wall.   I got up to look at it.   A
small bookshelf was close to it, and I began glanc-
ing at the books.   I wanted to lead Wilde on to
talk to me in a more serious vein.   I sat down
again, and rather timidly asked him if he had read
"Souvenirs de la Maison des Morts."

He gave me no direct answer, but began:—
"Russian writers are extraordinary.   What makes
their books so great is the pity they put into them.
You know how fond I used to be of "Madame Bo-
vary," but Flaubert would not admit pity into his
work, and that is why it has a petty and restrained
character about it.   It is sense of pity by means
of which a work gains in expanse, and by which
it opens up a boundless horizon.   Do you know,
my dear fellow, it was pity that prevented me from
killing myself?   During the first six months I was
dreadfully unhappy, so utterly miserable that I
wanted to kill myself, but what kept me from doing
so was looking at *the others,* and seeing that they
were as unhappy as I was, and feeling sorry for
them.   Oh, dear! what a wonderful thing pity is,
and I never knew it."

He was speaking in a low voice, without any excitement.

"Have you ever learned how wonderful a thing pity is? For my part I thank God every night; yes, on my knees I thank God for having taught it to me. I went into prison with a heart of stone, thinking only of my own pleasure, but now my heart is utterly broken—pity has entered into my heart. I have learned now that pity is the greatest and most beautiful thing in the world. And that is why I cannot bear ill-will towards those who caused my suffering and those who condemned me; no, nor to any one, because without them I should not have known all that. —— writes me terrible letters. He says he does not understand me, that he does not understand that I do not wish every one ill, and that every one has been horrid to me. No, he does not understand me. He cannot understand me any more. But I keep on telling him that in every letter: we cannot follow the same road. He has his, and it is beautiful —I have mine. His is that of Alcibiades; mine is now that of St. Francis of Assisi. Do you know St. Francis of Assisi? A wonderful man! Would you like to give me a great pleasure? Send me the best life of St. Francis you can find."

I promised it to him.   He went on:

"Yes, afterwards we had a charming prison Governor; oh! quite a charming man; but for the first six months I was dreadfully unhappy.   There was a Governor of the prison, a Jew, who was very harsh, because he was entirely lacking in imagination."

This last expression, spoken very quickly, was irresistibly funny; and, as I laughed heartily, he laughed too, repeated it, and then said:

"He did not know what to imagine in order to make us suffer.   Now, you shall see what a lack of imagination he showed.   You must know that in prison we are allowed to go out only one hour a day; then, we walk in a courtyard, round and round, one behind the other, and we are absolutely forbidden to say a word.   Warders watch us, and there are terrible punishments for any one caught talking.   Those who are in prison for the first time are spotted at once, because they do not know how to speak without moving their lips.   I had already been in prison six weeks and I had not spoken a word to anyone—not to a soul.

"One evening we were walking as usual, one behind the other, during the hour's exercise, when suddenly behind me I heard my name called.   It was the prisoner who followed me, and he said, 'Oscar Wilde, I pity you, because you must suffer more than we do.' Then I made a great effort not to be noticed (I thought I was going to faint), and I said without turning round, 'No, my friend, we all suffer alike.' And from that day I no longer had a desire to kill myself. We talked in that way for several days. I knew his name and what he had done. His name was P——; he was such a good fellow; oh! so good. But I had not yet learned to speak without moving my lips, and one evening—'C.3.3. (C.3.3. was myself) and A.4.8., step out of the ranks.'

"Then we stood out, and the warder said, 'You will both have to go before the Governor.' And as pity had already entered into my heart, my only fear was for him; in fact, I was even glad that I might suffer for his sake. But the Governor was quite terrible. He had P—— in first; he was going to question us separately, because you must know that the punishment is not the same for the one who speaks first, and for the one who answers: the punishment of the one who speaks first is double that of the other. As a rule, the first has fifteen days' solitary confinement, and the second has eight days only. Then the Governor wanted

to know which of us had spoken first, and naturally
P——, good fellow that he was, said it was he.
And afterwards, when the Governor had me in to
question me, I, of course, said it was I. Then the
Governor got very red because he could not understand it. 'But P—— also says that it was he who
began it. I cannot understand it. I cannot understand it.'

"Think of it, my dear fellow, he could *not* understand it. He became very much embarrassed and
said, 'But I have already given him fifteen days,'
and then he added, 'Anyhow, if that is the case, I
shall give you both fifteen days.' Is not that
extraordinary? That man had not a spark of imagination!"

Wilde was vastly amused at what he was saying,
and laughed—he was happy telling stories. "And,
of course," he continued, "after the fifteen days
we were much more anxions to speak to one another than before. You do not know how sweet
that is, to feel that one is suffering for another.
Gradually, as we did not go in the same order
each day, I was able to talk to each of the others,
to all of them, every one of them. I knew each
one's name and each one's history, and when each
was due to be released. And to each one I said,

'When you get out of prison, the first thing you must do is to go to the Post Office, and there you will find a letter for you with some money.' And so in that way I still know them, because I keep up my friendship with them. And there is something quite delightful in them. Would you believe it, already three of them have been to see me here? Is not that quite wonderful?

"The successor of the harsh Governor was a very charming man—oh! remarkably so—and most considerate to me. You cannot imagine how much good it did me in prison that 'Salomé' was being played in Paris just at that time. In prison, it had been entirely forgotten that I was a literary person, but when they saw that my play was a success in Paris, they said to one another, 'Well, but that is strange; he has talent, then.' And from that moment they let me have all the books I wanted to read. I thought, at first, that what would please me most would be Greek literature, so I asked for Sophocles, but I could not get a relish for it. Then I thought of the Fathers of the Church, but I found them equally uninteresting. And suddenly I thought of Dante. Oh! Dante! I read Dante every day, in Italian, and all through, but neither the 'Purgatorio' nor 'Paradiso' seemed written for me. It was his 'Inferno' above all that I read—could I help liking it? Cannot you guess? Hell, we were in it—Hell, that was prison!"

That same evening he told me a clever story about Judas, and of his proposed drama on Pharaoh. Next day he took me to a charming little house, about two hundred yards from the hotel, which he had rented and was beginning to furnish. It was there that he wanted to write his plays—his "Pharaoh" first, and then one called "Ahab and Jezebel" (he pronounced it "Isabelle"), which he related to me admirably.

The carriage which was to take me away was waiting, and Wilde got into it to accompany me part of the way. He began talking to me again about my book, and praised it, though with some slight reserve, I thought. At last the carriage stopped; he bade me good-bye, and was just going to get out, when he suddenly said, "Listen, my dear friend, you must promise me one thing. Your "Nourritures Terrestres" is good, very good, but promise me you will never write a capital 'I' again. And as I seemed scarcely to understand what he meant, he finished up by saying, "In Art, you see, there is no first person."

  *   *   *   *   *

And a short time afterwards Wilde went back to Paris.

His play was not written—it will never be written now. Society well knows what steps to take when it wants to crush a man, and it has means more subtle than death. Wilde had suffered too grievously for the last two years, and in too submissive a manner, and his will had been broken. For the first few months he might still have entertained illusions, but he soon gave them up. It was as though he had signed his abdication. Nothing remained in his shattered life but a mouldy ruin, painful to contemplate, of his former self. At times he seemed to wish to show that his brain was still active. Humour there was, but it was far-fetched, forced, and threadbare.

I met him again on two occasions only. One evening on the Boulevards, where I was walking with G——, I heard my name called. I turned round and saw Wilde. Ah! how changed he was! "If I appear again before writing my play, the world will refuse to see in me anything except the felon," he had once said to me. He had appeared again, without his play, and as he found certain doors closed in his face, he no longer sought admission anywhere. He prowled.

Friends, at different times, tried to save him. They did all they could think of, and were for taking him to Italy, but he eluded their efforts, and began to drift back. Among those who had remained faithful for the longest time, some had often told me that Wilde was no longer to be seen, and I was somewhat uneasy, I admit, at seeing him again, and, what is more, in a place where so many people might pass. Wilde was sitting at a table outside a café. He ordered two cocktails for G—— and myself. I was going to sit opposite to him in such a way as to turn my back to the passers-by, but Wilde noticed this movement, which he took as an impulse of absurd shame (he was not entirely mistaken, I must admit), and said, "Oh, sit here, near me," pointing to a chair at his side, "I am so much alone just now."

Wide was still well dressed, but his hat was not so glossy; his collar was of the same shape, but it was not so clean, and the sleeves of his coat were slightly frayed at the edges.

"When I used to meet Verlaine in days gone by," he continued with an outburst of pride, "I was never ashamed of being seen with him. I was rich, light-hearted, and covered with glory, but I felt that to be seen with him was an honour, even

when Verlaine was drunk." Then fearing to bore
G———, I think, he suddenly changed his mood,
tried to be witty and to make jokes. In the effort
he became gloomy. My recollections here are
dreadfully sad. At last my friend and I got up.
Wilde insisted on paying for the drinks, and I
was about to say good-bye, when he took me aside
and, with an air of great embarrassment, said in a
low voice, "I say, I must tell you, I am absolutely
without a penny."

Some days afterwards I saw him again, and for
the last time. I do not want to repeat more than
one word of our conversation. He told me of his
troubles, of the impossibility of carrying out, or
even of beginning a piece of work. Sadly I reminded him of the promise he had made not to
show himself in Paris without having finished one
book. "Ah!" I began, "why did you leave Berneval so soon, when you ought to have stayed there
so long? I cannot say that I am angry with you,
but———"

He interrupted me, laid his hand on mine, looked
at me with his most sorrowful look, and said, "You
must not be angry with *one who has been crushed.*"

*   *   *   *   *

Oscar Wilde died in a shabby little hotel in the

Rue des Beaux Arts. Seven persons followed the hearse, and even they did not all accompany the funeral procession to the end. On the coffin were some flowers and some artificial wreaths, only one of which, I am told, bore any inscription. It was from the proprietor of the hotel, and on it were these words: "A Mon Locataire."

So ends M. Gide's "Study." Oscar Wilde died in the arms of his landlord, M. Dupoirier, on November 30, 1900, and was buried in Bagneux Cemetery on the 3d of December following. His tomb bears the following inscription:

OSCAR WILDE

Oct. 16th, 1854   Nov. 30th, 1900

Verbis meis addere nihil audebant et
super illos stillabat eloquium meum.

—*Job* xxix, 22.

R.I.P.

Sherard thus describes Wilde's last days:

For months before he died he suffered from pains in the head. At the same time he was lashing his moribund energies by the use of alcohol. Dupoirier relates that he used to write all night, keeping his strength alive with brandy.

In the end the pains grew so intolerable that the doctors said that an operation would be necessary. But the operation threatened to be a very difficult one, for it was impossible to locate the exact spot where surgical treatment would benefit the patient. Only one of the great masters of surgery could be trusted, so the physicians said, with such an operation. A huge fee was mentioned as the amount that would probably be demanded by such a master. "Ah, well, then," said Oscar, "I suppose that I shall have to die beyond my means." "He must have suffered terribly," says Dupoirier, "for he kept raising his hands to his head to try and ease the torture. He cried out again and again. We used to put ice on his head. I was ever giving him injections of morphine." Robert Ross was with him at the end. That he brought a Roman Catholic priest to the dying man has already been recorded with a recognition of the kindness of the act. There was another friend also in attendance. But fate would have it that neither of the two was there when Oscar Wilde breathed his last. This was at two o'clock on the afternoon of 30th November, 1900. Dupoirier was holding him in his arms when he passed away.

Lady Wilde, Oscar Wilde's mother, and his brother died during the poet's incarceration. His wife, who had been separated from him, died a year after his release. He was survived by his two sons.

CHAPTER XI.

A LITERARY ESTIMATE.

Shortly after leaving Reading Gaol, Oscar Wilde wrote a pathetic letter pleading for the kindlier treatment of children in prison. It was published in *The Daily Chronicle* in May, 1897, under the head "The Case of Warder Martin." This attracted wide attention, and later he published another letter in the *Chronicle* (March, 1898) on the subject of cruelties in English prisons, which was headed: "Don't Read This if You Want to be Happy To-day." This letter was signed, "The Author of 'The Ballad of Reading Gaol.'" For meantime this remarkable ballad had appeared, the only notable contribution to literature that Wilde made after his release from prison, for the "De Profundis," though published after his release, was written during Wilde's incarceration. Of this ballad a leading London paper said:

"The whole is awful as the pages of Sophocles.

That he has rendered with his fine art so much of the essence of his life and the life of others in that inferno to the sensitive is a memorable thing for the social scientist, but a much more memorable thing for literature. This is a simple, a poignant, a great ballad, one of the greatest in the English language."

"The Ballad of Reading Gaol" was published early in 1898, and Wilde spent much time and labor in polishing and revising it. It is interesting to note at a glance some of the changes which Wilde made in his original copy of the ballad, as evidencing the care that he gave to each line, not considering so much the metrical effect as the value of the words. The following examples are taken from the original manuscript copy, kindly loaned to the publishers of this edition of Wilde's works by the possessor, a gentleman residing in New York City. The original copy is to be found in the interlineations:

> In Debtors' Yard the stones are hard,
>   And the dripping wall is high,
> So it was there he took the air
>   Beneath the leaden sky,
> And by each side a warder walked,

For fear the man might die.
For fear the man *would* die.

Or else he sat with those who watched
Or else he sat with *silent men*
  His anguish night and day;
  Who watched him night and day;
Who watched him when he rose to weep,
  And when he crouched to pray;
Who watched him lest himself should rob
  The scaffold of its prey.

The Governor was strong upon
The Governor was *strict* upon
  The Regulations Act:
  The Regulations *set:*
The Doctor said that Death was but
  A scientific fact:
And twice a day the Chaplain called
  And left a little tract.

Or else he might be moved, and try
Or else he might be moved, *or* try
  To comfort or console:
And what should Human Pity do
  Pent up in Murderers' Hole?
What word of grace in such a place
  Can help a brother's soul?

In a letter to his publisher, Mr. Leonard Smithers, Wilde says of the ballad: "The standard by which the poem is to be judged is not that of lyrical beauty, but of realistic presentation and actuality: at least by a sane critic, if there is one outside Bedlam."

The ballad has been translated into French, German and Spanish. Indeed, the European vogue of Wilde is everywhere spreading; in Germany and Italy especially, his influence upon the literature of the day is a dominant one. The Continent generally has opened its arms to the poet whom England rejected. But even in England, as well as in America, a Wilde revival is evident. Speaking of this the *Boston Transcript* recently said:

"Such renown as his could never have come to Oscar Wilde living. It comes to him dead freely and ungrudgingly and deservedly. His poems are read wherever the English language is spoken, his prose is becoming a model of the purest English style, his plays are acted with a full understanding of their great merit, and his books are sought by collectors and bibliographers."

But from across the water, from England itself,

a voice has been uplifted for Oscar Wilde which has spoken the best and sanest words yet uttered in defining his position in literature. In an article, quoted here in full, which appeared in the August, 1906, number of the *Westminster Review,* Mr. Wilfrid M. Leadman has this to say of "The Literary Position of Oscar Wilde." The article is reproduced here because it should be read by all readers of Wilde's works:

Maeterlinck has shown us in one of his admirable essays how impossible and how absurd it is to attempt to reconcile human affairs with the idea of an intelligent external justice impartially and invariably meting out good for good and evil for evil. All injustice springs originally from man himself, or from what we are pleased to call Nature. The intelligence of Nature is purely mechanical; she has smiles and frowns for both moral and immoral alike, without regard to character or conduct. The "justice" or "injustice" of man is purely arbitrary, hence its seeming inexplicability. In no sense, perhaps, is the cruelty and caprice of human justice shown more painfully than in the history of literature. Here and there, scattered over the globe, we find lonely and unrecognised geniuses whose messages have faded and remain forgotten because no one has been found to appreciate or to understand them. And too often the fault lay, not in the message or its deliverer, but in the world. On the other hand, we find writers (not always so deserving) concerning whose high position the world has spoken decisively. She has placed them on lofty pedestals. And those whom she chooses for this honour are usually the writers who have made a successful appeal to some strong force in human nature. They count their followers by millions; for they have a straightforward message for plain minds. True, in distant years their names may fade forever to make room for other names bearing similar messages, but, whatever their ultimate fate be, they have at least the satisfaction of present glory and the supreme consolation of being understood by their fellows. In the contemplation of these darlings of public opinion we feel no pain; but, when we turn to the victims of that same public opinion, we cannot but feel angered at the grotesque caprice of human justice. Among the writers so rejected by the world there are some whom she has spurned simply because she has not troubled to understand them. Prominent among this mournful group is Oscar

Wilde. Around that hapless man controversy incessantly played in the past and apparently will continue to play in the future. His whole literary work (plays, poems, essays, and fiction) in vain cried out for just criticism—prejudice, misconception, and a strained sense of respectability refused it. His few admirers were dubbed a senseless clique dazzled by the showy glitter of his language. Wilde was always considered a mere "poseur." Fault was found with all his writings. It was said that his prose was disfigured by incongruous ornament; his poetry was a feeble echo of Keats and Swinburne. His wonderful essays—especially "The Decay of Lying" and "The Soul of Man"—were admired only for their peculiar brilliance; their inherent depth of philosophy was overlooked. His plays were deemed conventional in construction and overloaded with spurious wit. Great and undue stress was invariably laid on the man's eccentricities; in the public eye Wilde was only a witty fellow yearning for celebrity and capable of performing weird literary antics to attain that object. He is indeed a tragic figure. Laughed at in his youth, misunderstood in his maturity, spurned in his closing years, accused of plagiarism, blamed for his love of posture, constantly charged

with artificiality, an object of unceasing attack
from pulpit and press—in a word, roundly abused
all his life—Wilde would seem to have small
chance, in this country, at any rate, of literary
fame. Long before the catastrophe of 1895 he had
an extraordinary amount of prejudice against him.
His downfall was the crowning condemnation. After that it looked as though he were indeed doomed
to an eternal outer darkness. And yet, leaving
the question of his conduct on one side, his sole
fault was simply his unswerving fidelity to his own
intellectual bias. He could not write about ordinary things in an ordinary way. He could not
present the British public with its favourite dish
of love and sport. He was incapable of moulding
his maxims on traditional conceptions of virtue
and vice. It was, perhaps, inevitable that the un-
educated British public should turn its back on
one who at almost every opportunity flaunted in
its face the most unusual doctrines. For it must
be confessed, Oscar Wilde enunciated doctrines utterly alien to the ingrained Puritanism and ath-
leticism of the English people. The man who runs
counter to national traditions and prejudices is
bound to provoke bitter hostility. The man who,
in this country, places art before muscle, or sets

the individual will above the conventional law, seems sure, sooner or later, to come to grief. Yet, in spite of his unpopularity, Wilde was never discouraged. Borne up by his own motto, "To be great is to be misunderstood," he moved steadily forward, and made his mark. True, his influence was limited to the very few, but it existed, and will expand further in the time to come. The unconventional will always thank him for his unflinching advocacy of things unconventional. The artist will remember him because he was one of the courageous few who helped to remove English theories of art from the tyranny of rigid tradition to the freedom of unfettered originality. He may have been rash, he may have been inclined to pose, his writings may show traces of plagiarism—an innocent sort of plagiarism that is almost a transformation—but there was always a thoroughness about his work which certainly deserved fairer consideration. To the average English mind his doctrines could only suggest the bizarre and the unnatural; but that was because the English mind had not yet learnt to appreciate an oblique point of view. Not that Wilde's outlook was always unusual. On the contrary, some of his short stories—especially "The Happy Prince," "The Star-Child," and "The

Model Millionaire"—though necessarily tinted with his peculiar colouring, would satisfy the most exacting moralist by their tone of "poetic justice." If Wilde occasionally trampled on cherished national convictions or sometimes thrust strangely hued flowers amongst our soberer blossoms, it was not from love of opposition; it was rather because he had to drift whither his fantastic and exuberant intellect listed.

Wilde's descent into the abyss seemed at the time to be the death-blow to what little influence he had already gained. The hasty verdict of a rather superficial morality said then that his influence must have been essentially unhealthy. From that time to the publication of "De Profundis," it was even deemed a breach of manners to allude to Wilde in any way. However, that interesting posthumous book has been the cause of a partial change of the public attitude. We are once more allowed to discuss Wilde's book without hearing a shocked "hush," or being suspected of loose views on moral matters. Whatever one's opinion may be as to the genuineness of the repentance shown in "De Profundis," one may at any rate be deeply thankful for what it has undoubtedly done toward the rehabilitation of its author. He is no longer under a ban. He may eventually receive a high place in English literature. After all, his admitted writings cannot fairly be deemed unhealthy. Those who see "an undercurrent of nasty suggestion" in some of his literary productions must surely be so obsessed by their knowledge of his unfortunate behaviour as to lose all power of disconnecting two absolutely independent things, namely, his art and his private life. The ludicrous charges of immorality brought against that book of painted words and lordly language, "Dorian Gray," fall to the ground at once when it is known that the book was written solely for money. As Mr. Sherard says in his "Life of Oscar Wilde," no author would risk the financial success of a book by filling it with immoral teachings. The marvel to me is that Wilde managed to produce such a transcendant work of art under the pressure of such a prosaic stimulus.

In the past, before his downfall, Wilde's works were only read carefully by a select few. Others, it is true, granted a certain momentary admiration to his prose, but it was the sort of admiration involuntarily and temporarily evoked by gorgeous fireworks rather than the lasting admiration felt for a permanent object of art. Now, if justice is to be done to any author's work the impersonal attitude is imperative. The intellectual reader must sink his personal predilections, he must not keep asking himself whether he agrees with this or that sentiment expressed by an author. It is not very hard to do. There are minds which dislike stories packed with scenes of love, but such minds need not on that account be debarred from appreciating the almost faultless love-scenes in "Richard Feverel." Of course, when the reader is by nature in perfect accord with the writer's sentiments, the enjoyment will be fuller and more satisfactory than when his appreciation be acquired; but in both cases the object of the writer's genius will have been attained. In the case of Wilde's works there is a real necessity for impartiality of standpoint, because only the few are by nature and inclination in tune with his work. The majority must learn to put themselves into tune. Two difficulties—broadly speaking—hamper anything like a general and intelligent recognition of Wilde's genius. The first is undoubtedly the moral obliquity or seeming moral obliquity revealed by the criminal trial of 1895. The second is the lack of effort or ability to understand Oscar Wilde's trend of thought. Would that the former might be for

ever forgotten! After all, his writings are of vastly more importance to posterity than his private
conduct. The stolid Englishman, however, finds it
hard to differentiate between a man's private character and his books. Certain unfortunate impressions received in 1895 cloud his honest judgment in
the matter of Wilde's position in literature. Now
this is not the place to discuss the pathological
aspect of Oscar Wilde's conduct, but I may be permitted to say that his restitution—to be permanent—must depend on a fuller knowledge of an
obscure branch of morbid pathology.

This, at present, for obvious reasons, is impossible. No doubt "De Profundis," with its confession
of humility and its partial admission of error, will
impress many minds favourably, but the more mat-
ter-of-fact minds care little whether that book be
entirely sincere or merely a huge pose intended to
transform public opinion. What they do care about
is a *locus standi* based on sound scientific grounds.
Once such a basis be generally accepted, perhaps
the worst obstacle to the recognition of Wilde will
have been taken away. Let it be admitted that
Wilde erred greatly; then charity reminds us that
there is such a thing as forgiveness of sin. Let it
be granted that pathological research will explain

and even excuse much of his conduct; common
sense will then bid us banish our rigid prudery and
consign once and for all to oblivion what really
has absolutely nothing to do with our unchecked
contemplation of a great artist.

The other obstacle to an unbiassed conception of
this writer's productions is not so easily defined as
that just discussed, for the latter sprang into existence at a definite time, whilst this one had existed ever since Wilde published his first book of
poems. From the beginning Wilde's ideas were
diametrically opposed to all our eminently respect-
able British traditions of art. The reading world
failed to grasp his meaning. And that was mainly
due to what one may call our national inability
to understand a creed whose keynote was the worship of beauty. We are, above all, a stolid race,
in no way over-attracted by beauty; we certainly
love personal cleanliness and comfort, but it is a
cleanliness derived from cold water rather than
from warm, and a comfort obtained from blankets
and brick rather than from silks and marble. We
cannot see the use of any one's making a fuss over
a beautiful thing simply because of its beauty.
Such a proceeding savours to us of lunacy or idola-
try. And when Wilde, in 1881, burst upon our

sober minds with his first book of poems—saturated as it was with a lavish, reckless admiration of beauty—we felt that here indeed was a strange apostle teaching a still stranger cult. Coming, as this book did, on the heels of Wilde's æsthetic campaign—after all, but a pardonable youthful extravagance, and, as Mr. Sherard points out, completely cured by that American tour, which taught a needed practical lesson—there was, perhaps, some reason for its hostile reception. "Here is a man," said the critics, "who values all glittering evanescence of a coloured bubble above morality itself." This sweeping opinion represented the belief of many critics at that time, and, unfortunately for Wilde, later events seemed confirmatory. In one sense possibly Wilde did set beauty above morality, but it was above the conventional conception of morality—that is something arbitrary and too often uncharitable—*not* above goodness. In any case, one must not base one's conception of Wilde's attitude toward morality on anything which he has written. Some men do, indeed, project their own personalities into their books, in spite of Wilde's dictum: "To reveal art and to conceal the artist is the true aim of art. The artist can express everything." But one may be confident that the author of "Dorian Gray" has been guilty of no such literary soul-dissecting. An intimate friend of his—a man, perhaps, more fitted to speak authoritatively on this subject than any other man living—told me that Wilde only revealed *one* aspect of his own character in his books, and that not the most attractive aspect.

Read in the clear light of intelligent criticism, the first book of poems teaches only one thing, namely, that here is an author almost unique in his whole-hearted worship of form and colour, a worship, too, that is not casual, capricious, and superficial, but serious, terribly serious, and thoroughly healthy. Of course, all this was horribly unpractical, and most Englishmen, with their innate dislike of "hollow beauty," shrugged their shoulders. Wilde, in his first as in his later efforts, wrote only for minds attuned to his. Others must take the right attitude or else pass on elsewhere.

Wilde has plainly this to his credit, that he never tried to win the public, never debased the art of literature by pandering to any popular movement. Of that exquisite set of allegories, "The House of Pomegranates," he finely said (in answer to some mystified critics) that "it was intended neither for the British child nor for the British public." Indeed, some think that much, if not all, of his work was the accidental, irresponsible, yet irresistible overflow of an ever creative intellect, and not literature written with any definite purpose. On this question, however, it is better to keep an open mind.

Wilde had an inherent horror of the commonplace, and this seems to have led him occasionally into a rather strained effort after a rather petty kind of originality. Of course his numerous enemies laid hold of that habit and made it the foundation of a great deal of silly abuse. Frivolous, frothy remarks put into the mouths of some of Wilde's characters were solemnly quoted as part of Wilde's creed. Witty repartees deliberately torn from their proper context in his plays were seriously construed as Wilde's own gospel. The words of few men have undergone such distortion and misinterpretation as have those of this genius. One can only be thankful that now at any rate there are signs of the advent of Truth, there are signs of a strong, fresh breeze sweeping away those murky mists and grotesque masks that have so long hidden the real Wilde. It is at last dawning on men's minds that his writings are not so much external ornament concealing a blank void, and that his wit is often wisdom, only occasionally nonsense. Some critics say that Wilde's art may be very entertaining and very clever, but that (with the exception of "De Profundis") it leads us nowhere. But is that, even if true, a sound objection to his work? For some people, at any rate, it is refreshing to step aside from the hustle and bustle of literary missionaries and to enjoy a healthy rest with an author who does not burden his readers with any tedious lesson. As a matter of fact, whether Wilde had any fixed aim or not, his work most certainly points—and points clearly—to a definite goal. I think that there are those who will say that they have been led by this author to very fruitful regions. If some people feel that Wilde only takes them a giddy dance over tracts of glittering but useless beauty, there are others who feel that his restless flights helped them to realise the wonder of much that previously seemed common and graceless. What, pray, are many of Wilde's short stories, such as the "Young King" and "The Happy Prince," but artistically embroidered pleas for social reform? Who can read "Dorian Gray" intelligently without hearing the deep bass note of doom, at first faint, but gradually growing louder and louder amid the brilliant cascade of frivolous treble notes, till it drowns them in the final crash of just punishment for error? Can any one fail to note the stern moral lesson of "Salomé"? Who can study his other plays carefully without learning the superb philosophy of human life that runs through them like a silver thread amid a many-hued skein? And who can help observing the high aspirations which lift so much of his verse out of the sphere of mere decorated rhyme? The truth is, Wilde's work bristles with moral advice, but—partly owing to his own oft-repeated condemnation of stories with a moral, and partly owing to the innate obtuseness of most of his readers—it is constantly overlooked.

In the early nineties Wilde's position was almost unique; he was looked upon as a literary phenomenon defying satisfactory solution. His art bewildered, amazed, repelled; if a few here hailed him as worthy to rank with intellectual giants, a multitude there said his art was unreal, frothy, and sometimes dangerous. He was a kaleidoscope puzzle even to his own friends. This is shown by the impressions of him recorded by various personal friends; they all seemed to see a different man: none of their presentations agree. Still, Wilde kept on his way, gyrating giddily onward. His art must sooner or later bear fruit and find its home; such ability could not be destined to be wasted. Then, just as he seemed on the point of grasping honour and glory, there came in his career that fatal crisis, the one bright spot in which was, perhaps, that it saved him from worse things. Prison life steadied him. It helped him to take a fuller, broader view of life, to recognise how incomplete had been his former life when it confined itself to the enjoyment of this world's splendour and refused to acknowledge or share in the world's sorrow. In the quiet of his cell he could write the pleading, passionate prose afterwards given us as "De Profundis." This book has struck the public imagination. And to me, of all the puzzling problems connected with the unfortunate Oscar Wilde, none is so inexplicable as this. A book, the keynote of which is an abject, almost grovelling, humility, has captivated the hearts of a people whose chief characteristics are sturdiness and independence of character. It may seem a dreadful statement, but if I were asked to name any book by Wilde that was not quite healthy in tone, I should promptly mention "De Profundis." At the same time, I should hasten to add that the unhealthy part of the book was the unavoidable outcome of the author's terrible position. The crushed must needs be very humble.

But, apart from that one demoralising note of excessive humility, "De Profundis" is a splendid progression of noble thoughts leading in very truth from the dank gutter to the gleaming stars. The price paid for its evolution by the author was awful, but, as a writer said recently in the *Hibbert Journal,* it may have been absolutely necessary. Both this book and "A Ballad of Reading Gaol" fill the gaps left in Oscar Wilde's earlier work—gaps which might have remained empty but for his downfall. Neither of these books is, perhaps, any real advance (from a purely literary point of view) on his former work. But because they are both serious, both more in accordance with the tastes of the "man in the street," they have effected a considerable change in the public attitude. It would be safe to say that Wilde's literary position was never less insecure than at the present time. The favourable reception awarded to his last two books has opened the door to a more sensible and fairer examination of all his books. And that is all we admirers of Wilde's genius demand. The rest— the eventual granting to Wilde of a niche in the temple of English literature—will follow in due course. Some of his work already smacks of "the day before yesterday," it is true; but much of it is imperishable, capable of standing the test of ages. Much of it represents some of the finest prose-poetry in our language. Oscar Wilde was our *one* English artist in words.

At length a turning-point has been reached. Oscar Wilde is once more on trial, but it is a trial whose result can involve no disgrace, but which may—surely will—bring him a radiant wreath of fame. It will last long, for there is a strong array of witnesses on either side, and there is much up-hill work for his advocates. The scarlet flame of his disgrace still throws a lurid light on all his literary works, but it has begun to grow paler and smaller, and ere long it may become extinct, and in its place will dazzle forth the jewelled light of his undying intellect, teaching our descendants about the eternity of beauty and joy, but bidding them never forget the temporary reign of pain and sorrow, beseeching them to sweep away the tainted refuse that hides the crystal purity below, asking them for justice. And will not these requests be granted? On the Continent, in America, the great awakening has begun; there, the genius has triumphed over the convict, the sinner has been lost in the artist. Must it be said, then, by a later generation that Britain alone never forgave the strange errors of one of her brightest thinkers, but was content to let foreign hands raise him and his from the mire? Surely no; surely we are not so rich in intellectual wealth that we can afford to pass *any* of our artists by "on the other side."

Anyhow, when the haze of Time has finally covered all trace of the human frailties of Oscar Wilde, his genius, now slowly forcing its way upward through many a clogging obstacle, will rise resplendent and glorious before the eyes of an understanding posterity.

THE END.